TO PROCLAIM YOUR FAITHFULNESS

ואמונתך בלילות

TO PROCLAIM YOUR FAITHFULNESS
A Young Widow's Notebook

Brachah (Chubara) Ben-Mashiach

Translated from the Hebrew
by Miriam Samsonowitz

FELDHEIM PUBLISHERS
JERUSALEM NEW YORK

Originally published in Hebrew as *Ve'emunatecha Baleilot*.

The author can be reached at POB 7318, Jerusalem, Israel, or at telefax 972-2-566-9696.

First published 2004

ISBN 1-58330-698-6

Copyright © 2004 by Brachah Ben-Mashiach

All rights reserved.
No part of this publication may be translated, reproduced, stored in a retrieval system or transmitted, in any form or by any means, electronic, mechanical, photocopying, recording, or otherwise, without permission in writing from the publishers.

FELDHEIM PUBLISHERS
POB 43163 / Jerusalem, Israel

208 Airport Executive Park
Nanuet, NY 10954

www.feldheim.com

10 9 8 7 6 5 4 3 2 1

Printed in Israel

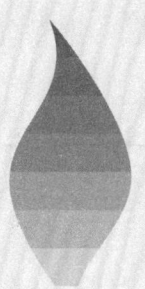

*A memorial candle
in commemoration of
the noble soul
of the father of my children*

Tzion Chubara zt"l

עובדיה יוסף
הראשון לציון
ונשיא מועצת חכמי התורה

ב"ה

OVADIA YOSSEF
RISHON LEZION
AND PRESIDENT OF TORAH SAGES COUNSIL

SALEM _____   ירושלים _____

הסכמה

היה למראה עיני הספר "ואמונתך בלילות" מאת הגב' ברכה בן משיח שתחי'. רשימות שכתבה לחזק את לבה, מתוך מכתבי עידוד וחיזוק שכתב בעלה המנוח בעת אשר שכב על ערש דווי, אפוף יסורים ומכאובים, מרים וקשים, מתוך קבלת דין שמים באהבה. והם הדברים שכתבה בדם לבה ובדמע, לחזק את לבה באמונה בבורא עולם, אשר בידו נפש כל חי, ובאמונה בחיי העולם הבא, העתיד הנצחי.

ומגו דזכי לנפשה, הוציאה לאור ספר זה, לחזק לבבות שבורים ובעלי יסורים, לבל יפלו ברוחם. וגם יש בו כדי לחזק ולעורר את זיק האמונה הטמונה בלב. איישר חילה לאורייתא.

ויהי רצון שתשא "ברכה" מאת ה', לאורך ימים ושנות חיים, בטוב ובנעימים, בבריאות איתנה ונהורא מעלייא, ותרוה נחת מבניה, ואחריתה תסגה.

Approbation

I HAVE SEEN THE BOOK *VeEmunatcha BaLeilot* by Mrs. Brachah Ben-Mashiach, which is composed of journal entries that the author wrote in order to strengthen her heart. It also includes messages of encouragement and determination that her deceased husband wrote on his sickbed, when he was overcome by afflictions and pain, yet accepted the Heavenly judgment with love. She wrote these words while the wound was fresh, and tears were in her eyes, to strengthen her heart with faith in our Creator Who controls the lives of all, and with faith in the World to Come, the world of eternal life.

She is now publishing this book to encourage those who are broken-hearted and to lift up the spirits of those suffering afflictions. The book also fortifies and arouses faith in Hashem deep in one's heart.

May she be blessed by Hashem with a long life, blessing, comfort, good health, and spiritual elevation. May she have *nachat* from her children and may her future be exalted.

Ovadia Yossef

Contents

Preface to the English Edition x

From the Preface to the New Hebrew Edition. xi

Foreword by Rav Mordechai Neugraschel xiii

Introduction by Amiel Ben-Mashiach xvii

Prologue. xix

Vindicating Hashem's Judgment. 1

When Shivah Ends 41

Stories about Tzion *zt"l* 121

How Does One Overcome?. 139

Epilogue. 165

Glossary 167

Preface to the English Edition

THIS EDITION HAS BEEN published in response to many requests from both organizations and individuals regarding the great need in our generation for the message it contains. Therefore, I undertook this project as an expression of my great esteem for my wife Brachah, who has become a sympathetic friend to hundreds of widows and orphans, guiding them with wisdom and sensitivity and encouraging them to take their bereavement and sorrow and turn them into a powerful force for living creative lives. Many have learned from her not to perpetuate their suffering and its consequences into the next generation.

One woman's strength and determination has created a network of workshops and emotional support for widows and orphans, in which the emphasis is independence, not dependence. Only one who has known the depths of such pain can work for the emotional recovery and "return to life" of others who are still overwhelmed and incapacitated by it.

Concerning *tziduk ha-din*, acknowledging the rightness of Divine judgment, Rabbi Meir HaLevi Abulafia, *zt"l*, who lost a son and a daughter in his lifetime, writes: "I thank Hashem that He let me gain control over my spirit and my evil inclination… to desire the desires of Hashem — that He guides me in His ways; and I will thank Him for both the good and the bad…. I trust in God, I will praise His word (*Tehillim* 56:11). I will vindicate the Judgment."

"Look, I have put before you *today* — life, and the good; and death, and the evil…*and you shall choose life*" (*Devarim* 30:15,19).

May this English edition be an *ilui neshamah* for Victoria bat Zehava, of blessed memory, the mother of my children.

Amiel Ben-Mashiach
26 Av 5764
the twentieth Yahrtzeit of Tzion Chubara, *zt"l*

From the Preface to the New Hebrew Edition

WHEN HARAV HAGAON RAV SHLOMO ZALMAN AUERBACH, *zt"l*, told us to publish this book, we had no idea where it would lead.

Nine years have passed since then, thousands of copies of this book have been printed, and many have been donated to bereaved families and to organizations such as Lev l'Achim, Ezer m'Tzion, and Arachim.

In describing my own suffering and laying bare our private lives, the words have reached the hearts of our fellow Jews searching for a direction and a path.

To our anguish, the sorrowful reality of our times has brought thousands of responses, and almost every widow has exclaimed: "I feel as if I wrote this book!" or "It is as if this book were written just for me."

Our book has touched not only widows, but all those whose suffering has tormented them with questions of the whys, wherefores, and hows of Hashem's Divine judgment.

This book attempts to give answers to those questions. And what is the answer at its purest, most fundamental level?

As long as the *Beit HaMikdash*, Hashem's Holy Temple, lies in ruins, we are not able to dwell in tranquility.

As long as the People of Israel are divided in their hearts, as long as we cannot manage to unite, we cannot demand Redemption.

With this book, we hope to provide a ray of hope which will enable people to continue living a purposeful life, a life of meaning. For when we understand the meaning of suffering, we find both a direction and a path.

I would like to acknowledge:

- the Creator of the World, Who has brought us this far,

- my late father, *zt"l*, and my dear mother, *t"l*, who have been pillars of faith and strength for me,
- my husband Amiel, whose light illuminates my way,
- and my wonderful children, who took an active part in this endeavor.

Brachah Ben-Mashiach
Tishrei 5764

Foreword

by Rav Mordechai Neugraschel shlita

BRACHAH'S STORY WILL UNDOUBTEDLY be read with bated breath and many tears, tears that will surely find favor with the King Who is appeased with tears. After a preliminary reading — and after the inevitable emotional catharsis has dissipated — it should be read again, a second and a third time. This book should not be read casually, but carefully studied and heeded. This is not just a story of one woman's struggle and her vitality, majestic faith, trust in Hashem, and vindication of His judgment. It is an exceptional testimony full of sensitivity and profundity, which can help everyone who needs strengthening in faith and trust in our Creator — and who doesn't? It is especially significant for one whose life has not been a bed of roses, who has been called to take up the banner, to demonstrate his fidelity even in the hardest of times.

I want to make it absolutely clear that I am not writing an approbation. I am not a person to engage in such grand things. However, I went through a similar crisis in my youth, when my family and I drank the bitter cup of losing my father *z"l* who passed away young after a difficult illness, leaving my mother a young widow with small children. Since those days when we witnessed my father's indescribable suffering, which he bore with supreme courage, my heart gravitated to the dilemma of the righteous who suffer and the wicked who prosper" in general, and to the meaning of suffering in particular. Because of this, my heart urged me to add a few words to the heartfelt work in front of us.

Our Sages mention three parables concerning the suffering of the righteous. Each of these parables refers to a different kind of suffering.

One parable involves a potter who sells clay pots. To publicize the good quality of his pots, he bangs on them. On which pots does he bang? Obviously on the sturdiest pots.

Another parable concerns a flax-seller who is combing his flax. Which flax will he comb? Obviously the best quality flax.

The last parable involves a man who has two cows. Which cow does he yoke to the plow? Obviously the stronger cow.

There are righteous individuals whom HaKadosh Baruch Hu afflicts to sanctify His Name in public, and to show the entire world how their sufferings only strengthen their belief. Trials of this kind can only be sent upon individuals with strong convictions. This is like the potter who bangs on sturdy pots to prove their resilience. He wouldn't bang on a weak pot, because he knows it would break.

There are righteous individuals whom Hashem afflicts in order to purify them, so they will reach the Next World in a perfect state. Only the righteous are allowed this kind of purification, and lesser individuals are not. Similarly, the flax-seller will not invest his time combing inferior flax which might split and, in any event, isn't worth his efforts to improve it.

And then there are righteous individuals whom Hashem afflicts in order to atone for their generation. Since they know how to accept suffering, their relatively small amount of suffering can atone for a large amount of evil. Were the wicked forced to suffer what they deserve, a sea of suffering would descend upon the world. Sometimes we merit seeing how suffering can lift the one who is afflicted, as well as those around him, to a supreme spiritual height.

However, we must remember that, although we can have this general understanding of the dilemma of a righteous man's sufferings and a wicked man's bliss, we can never know the fine details or the reasons why any particular person was given the suffering he was. At most, we can understand the basic principles (Ramchal, beginning of *Da'as Tevunos*). Our Sages taught us many different reasons why sufferings come upon a person, but nevertheless, one can never know for sure why a certain righteous man experiences hardship, or why a certain wicked man has a pleasant life.

Whatever befalls a person during his life in the corridor of This World is intended to strengthen him, to fortify his heart and prepare him for true life, which is a life of Torah and mitzvot in This World, and eternal life in the World to Come.

I wish the author the following: May your reward be that your worthy words serve as a mouthpiece for the feelings of many.

May this book provide *nachat* to Tzion *zt"l* who is as if speaking to us from the grave.

Introduction
by Amiel Ben-Mashiach

THESE DIARY PAGES WERE WRITTEN during the most difficult moments of a genuine trial, when the question of all questions, "Why do the righteous suffer," was confronting the author and demanding an answer. They were written as the events unfolded, out of an inner need rather than for publication. Today, after the *gaon* Rav Shlomo Zalman Auerbach *zt"l* gave his blessing, and after many others added their encouragement, these pages have been bequeathed to the public in fulfillment of our Sages' exhortation (*Berachos* 12) "to help one's fellow man with his burden."

In these pages, the reader will discover how to come to grips with bereavement, mourning, and the suffering that accompanies a tragedy. When a person passes away, an abyss breaks open. An empty hole is created and the whole world that was once familiar seems shrouded in a dark haze.

These pages of faith describe the way to deal courageously with life in the days during a mortal illness, before bereavement; as well as during the mourning period and afterwards. It is one's *emunah* in Hashem which helps rolls back the darkness in the face of light, amidst understanding and accepting Hashem's way with love.

"It is preferable to go to the house of a mourner... so that the *living* will take it to heart." This was said concerning one whose heart is still living, still awake, not one who is apathetic and unfeeling. For if one's heart has, God forbid, stopped believing and trusting in Hashem, one's life is not even considered life.

Mourning — but not despair!
One must fight against the feeling of despair, and chase it away before it waylays a person from life's realities and prevents him from serving Hashem in joy.

Crying — but not self-mortification!
To cry — yes! One must cry! It is mentioned in *Yalkut Shimoni* (*Bereishis, Vayera* 22) that during *Akeidat Yitzchak*, Avraham Avinu wept until he was totally inundated in tears. Yitzchak also wept heartrendingly. One should not smother or deny one's nature.

King David turned to nature and asked it, "What is with you, O sea, that you flee; Yarden, that you turn backward?" (*Tehillim* 114:5). The answer was: "The earth quakes before the Master."

The recitation of Kaddish expresses our vindication of Hashem's judgment. Despite our suffering, we exalt and sanctify HaKadosh Baruch Hu.

A Jew should and must believe in every situation that "He has put a stop to darkness" (Job 25:3). It is mentioned in the name of the holy Zohar (*Tetzaveh* 184a) that "the darker it is, the more important is the light that breaks through." One prayer that breaks through darkness and haze is more important than a hundred prayers said in ordinary times.

When is it dark? At the hour before dawn. There is no time darker than that.

Life is a wondrous gift which Hashem gave mankind. However, it is finite. We shouldn't regard it frivolously, but should try to fulfill our life's mission as perfectly as possible.

"I will sing to the Eternal while I live; I will sing praise to my God while I exist" (*Tehillim* 104:33).

Prologue

OUR LIFE ON EARTH IS A PUZZLE. We are twisted by the vicissitudes of our destiny, swinging back and forth, going up and down. What do we know about our lives? Where do they begin and where do they end? What is the potential of "me" in the immense expanse of the universe? Are we even allowed to ask ourselves these questions? Sometimes yes, and sometimes no.

But one day something happens. Something that stops the racing wheel of life and tells you, "Think! You are frittering away your time."

If so, what is life?

I tried to answer questions such as these in the diary I wrote for my children beginning from the day when I realized that they would be orphans. I knew the day would come when they would ask questions.

Unvoiced questions are also questions. I didn't want these questions to remain unanswered. I therefore felt it was my duty and privilege to write down these chapters in my diary for their sake.

I want to mention that some pages took me weeks to write because my hands shook so badly.

I didn't plan to publish this diary, but then something happened to me on Erev Yom Kippur of this year which I couldn't ignore.

The atmosphere in the country was morbid because of the terrible slaughter that was taking place; Jewish blood was being shed regularly. The question, "What can be done?" tore me apart. I prayed to the Creator of the Universe on behalf of each individual person, asking Him to enlighten our hearts to know and seek the truth.

And then I asked, as one person asks another, "Ribono shel Olam! How can a little person like me help? If I only knew how...."

And then, in the morning, before I got up to pray the Yom Kippur

Shacharit service, I had a dream. In the dream, a distinguished rabbi who had lived 200 years ago appeared. He was traveling swiftly in the direction of Eastern Europe. I clearly saw gorgeous scenes of verdant hills, as if Jerusalem had been dipped in green.

I felt a sense of security, a peace of mind I had never felt before.

And then I called out, "What is this *tzaddik* doing in our house? He passed away so long ago!"

I called out the name of the *tzaddik*, and he telepathically commanded me to remain silent. He ordered me not to mention his name. "Only you see me," he said.

The door opened by itself. He entered, and stood at the foot of the bed where the *gaon* Rav Shlomo Zalman Auerbach *zt"l* (who, sorrowfully, has since passed away) was lying, very ill. For some unexplained reason, Rav Shlomo Zalman was staying in our house in my dream. The *tzaddik* blessed him agitatedly. Rav Shlomo Zalman turned to him and said, "Bless this woman also."

The figure blessed me and said, "You write words of truth which you must publish. Why aren't you publishing them to benefit the public?" His movements were sharp, quick, and clear. Telepathically, he indicated the top left drawer in my room, and immediately afterwards disappeared as he had come.

I immediately woke up. It was 5:40 A.M.

I clearly remembered every detail of the dream, except the name of the *tzaddik*. I was very much shaken. I woke my youngest son (he was the only one in the house at the time) and told him the contents of the dream. Afterwards, we hurried off to synagogue.

Right after Yom Kippur, I approached the top left drawer in my room, opened it, and discovered the declaration accepting Hashem's judgment which I had made as I stood over the fresh grave of my children's father on the very day of his funeral.

This dream gave me no peace. I didn't know what to do. Should I relate to the whole incident as merely a passing fantasy, or should I relate to it more seriously?

I kept the incident in my heart for a month, but my concern about it didn't diminish.

Rav Shlomo Zalman Auerbach's well-being also concerned me, because in my dream I had clearly seen he was very ill. I was especially concerned about the behest of the unnamed *tzaddik*, his sharp look, and his perceptiveness. I kept thinking about his words of rebuke, "Why aren't you publishing your writings?!"

I collected what I had written, and headed for the home of Rav Auerbach's son, Rav Baruch Auerbach *shlita*. I asked him to read the diary and answer my questions. HaRav HaGaon Baruch Auerbach read it and brought the main points before Rav Shlomo Zalman. The answer was, "The material is worthy of publication, because it can strengthen one's *emunah*." I was fortunate enough to receive Rav Shlomo Zalman's blessing before he passed away.

Afterwards, I showed the writings to my children, and asked their permission to publish the passages concerning them. They graciously agreed to the publication of all the material.

I decided to publish my journal as it was, without making any changes.

The journal was written sometimes forthrightly and sometimes in a roundabout way, depending on how I felt each day.

Since I wanted the diary to convey my feelings as they were at the time, I didn't edit it or embellish the style. Sometimes the diary seems to jump or skip sections, and events do not appear in their chronological order. Again, my mood dictated what I wrote and when. Since I'm not a professional writer, I apologize for any mistakes in composition and grammar. I did embellish the book with lovely quotes which I found in Simcha Raz's book, *Pitgamei Chassidim* (Chassidic Sayings). My thanks to him for that.

I owe special thanks to HaRav HaGaon Rav Baruch Auerbach and his wife *shlita*, and to Rav Mordechai Neugraschel and his wife *shlita*, who encouraged me to publish the book.

Thanks are also due to my daughter Ruthi, who did the graphics for the Hebrew edition of the book.

And above all, my dear husband Amiel, who with rare devotion continues to lead the household, and because of whom my children again merited a father who disburses spiritual leadership and true love. When I was preparing the book for publication, and at times found myself wavering, his encouragement spurred me on. I am thankful to all of you.

Now that I am bringing the book before the public, I have mixed feelings:

- Prayer and hope to the Master of the Universe that no mishap occur and no one be led astray through me.
- A demand of myself, after my heart was inspired to go this far, to continue carrying on...

Who am I to decide whether these words are worthy of being hidden away or publicized? I have therefore accepted the decision of the great *posek*, the *gaon* Rav Shlomo Zalman Auerbach *zt"l*, and in the merit of his blessing, may this offering of a simple woman, this *minchat oni*, be considered a sweet-smelling offering before Hashem.

As Rav Yisrael of Kuznitz said, "When the entire Jewish nation will give each other a hand, the hands will combine into one hand which will reach the Throne of Glory."

Amen, may it be so.

Brachah Ben-Mashiach
Nissan 5755

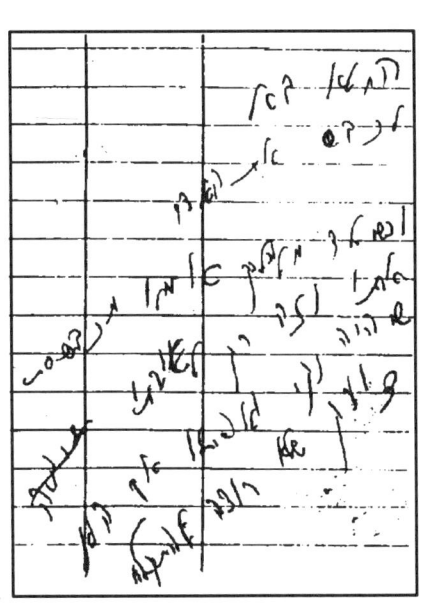

Vindicating Hashem's Judgment

I will vindicate Hashem's judgment
Even if it is too fearful to describe;
If the timing is distressing,
If the bitterness is great,
I will vindicate Hashem's judgment.

I CRIED OUT THESE WORDS as I stood beside the fresh grave of my children's father, the mainstay of my family, that Friday.

Afterwards, I began to write things down. I poured out all the moaning and clamoring of my heart onto the page. I poured out my children's cries of anguish. I collected stories about my husband from both great and ordinary people — stories that came out in the course of conversations, casually, without embellishment. I listened and wrote them down.

May this book serve as a memorial for my younger children, who never had the chance to learn directly from their father.

May it be a testimony for a six-month-old baby who only knew the light of his father's face from a printed picture. "This is Abba?" he asked when he was two, and threw the picture aside. I had to stand firm as steel to deal with the heavy burdens that fell on me all at once.

In the middle of the night, out on the balcony, when I couldn't fall asleep, I searched for the path of light that my mainstay had left behind. Thrown asunder from him and snatched away from a tranquil existence, I wandered, groping in the dark, seeking to vindicate the judgment.

I so much wanted to feel close to my Creator, but sometimes I felt so distant from Him. Sometimes I felt so abandoned by Hashem, so forsaken. I tried to grasp at any fragile thread that would tie me to HaKadosh Baruch Hu. I tried to find a staff to lean on, but every staff I tried was broken. I had to find support from within.

So I decided it was time to fulfill the charge that Tzion *zt"l* had given me: to read extensively about faith and trust in God.

The letters he had written during his last twenty-eight days, as he struggled with death in the Intensive Care Unit, provided a source of faith for me then, when my life changed so completely.

Our whole life by then had become notes written on paper and read. We read words, and we read each other's faces.

He couldn't speak that entire dreadful month, connected as he was by dozens of wires to miracle machines that monitored and recorded his body's functioning, in addition to having an inflated feeding tube and a respiratory tube stuck into his mouth. Sometimes, when the connections were loosened, he was able to write. From what he wrote we learned what was transpiring in his soul.

I will never know why his senses sharpened as his sufferings intensified. How did it happen that, contrary to medical opinion and to everyone's surprise, Tzion didn't pass away after two days, but, fully conscious, fought death valiantly for twenty-eight days? I want to speak about all this and more.

Erev Rosh Chodesh Av 5744 (1984)

YISRAEL FINISHED SAYING HAVDALAH, and Tzion hurried toward the bathroom. I heard him coughing. Taking my time, I bid farewell to the guests who had been with us for *seudah shelishit*, expecting Tzion to join me momentarily. But when I saw that he wasn't coming, I hurried to him.

The scene I saw was terrifying. He was coughing up quantities of blood.

I hugged him and whispered, "It will be okay, *b'ezrat Hashem*. I'll call the doctor right away." He stumbled to the bedroom and fell onto the bed, while I called Dr. Jacobson. Tzion spoke with him. Dr. Jacobson told him he would meet him immediately in Shaare Zedek hospital. He walked down the stairs, supported by his brothers.

We drove over.

Dr. Jacobson moved fast. Tzion had lost a lot of blood. Dr. Jacobson planned to stop the bleeding by inserting an inflated nasal tube into the windpipe to press on the tracheal veins. At the same time, he gave him a transfusion of four pints of blood. A light mood came over Tzion, and he said to Dr. Jacobson, "By us Yemenites, the custom is to afflict ourselves only during the week in which Tisha b'Av falls." Dr. Jacobson smiled grimly and said, "I'm treating you according to the Ashkenazic custom, where we afflict ourselves already from Rosh Chodesh."

We spent a difficult, tense night.

In the morning, Dr. Jacobson decided to check the windpipe, since the findings showed that the bleeding hadn't worsened. He took out the nasal tube, but Tzion immediately began to bleed. He took advantage of the short break, however, and stood up to pray. Dr. Jacobson insisted on inserting the nasal tube into the windpipe again, but Tzion begged him, "Please! Let me finish praying." Dr. Jacobson relented, and Tzion prayed.

Dr. Jacobson asked me to leave the room and go out to the corridor. The sound of my husband's groans reached my ears and seared my body. Gripping the *siddur* that Tzion had given me after we were engaged, I tried to extinguish the flames. I read the words, written in my fiancé's hand, the traditional scribal script in black ink. It said in Hebrew acrostic, spelling out my name:

To Brachah,

Understand the years of each generation;
Keep far away from the generation's futilities.
Direct your prayers to Jerusalem
And Hashem will lift His Face to you.

Tzion

I studied each word, and felt the warm sensation from that fresh, lovely period in which our affection for each other began to blossom. Wasn't it only yesterday?

The passage of time astonished me. I gathered all the scenes into a small ribbon of memories in my mind, where I could hear the sweet voice of my beloved Tzion and could be carried above my present turmoil to a happier world that existed between yesterday and tomorrow... as I wondered at the blue expanse of the heavens, searching for that channel of time, I decided I had one choice: no wavering between the different paths. Either be religious, and believe and rely on the Creator of the world — or abandon it all. No half-choices. Whatever you do, do it all the way!

So which way do I go? I heard the cry rising inside of me. Where to?

The vision of my six children passed in front of my eyes.

"Please! Watch over him and us," I prayed to my Creator.

🙠   🙠   🙠

I LOOKED THROUGH THE BOOK of *Tehillim* and my eyes fell on the verse: "Cast upon the Eternal your burden and He will sustain you" (55:23). At that moment, my brother-in-law Shalom arrived. "I've just come from Rav Kadouri," he said. "He asked me to tell you the verse, 'Cast upon the Eternal your burden and He will sustain you.'" I folded my arms, letting Hashem take my burden, and completely understood.

More time passed. Suddenly, Sheila, an old friend of ours, arrived. She had helped Tzion in the Intensive Care Unit. When he woke up, he wrote,

> There is a small book in the closet.

Sheila took out the book *Nefesh HaChaim* and began to read, but didn't understand. Tzion then wrote:

> Sin comes to cleanse a person. When a child is dirty, the mother washes him. It's only for his own good, so he'll be clean. Even if he screams that he doesn't want to take a shower.

Oh, how my Tzion justified the Heavenly judgment throughout his terrible sufferings!

I too am in Your hands, I told Hashem silently, and I will keep praying.

Night fell.

4 Av 5744 (1984)

THE INTENSIVE CARE UNIT is so frightening and silent. No sound but the beeping of machines and my husband's heavy breathing.

How lovely the nurses look in white. Like ministering angels, helping fate along.

I went outside. The heavens were wrapped in a gown of black with shining stars. The moon shone a whitish, bright light, and gazed at me tranquilly, as if to ask, "Why is today different from all other days?"

"No different! It's no different at all!" I replied. "All this will yet pass! It can't be otherwise!"

At home, I picked up my youngest child and held him close. My dear baby! No more sweet mother's milk. From now on, milk from a bottle.

His beautiful black eyes looked at me and asked, why?

I have no answer! Do you understand?

When the little ones woke up, they asked in a commotion, "Did Abba come home yet?"

"No, no, my dear children! Abba is sick, and all we can do is pray!"

From now on, days and nights without sleep, saying to myself, "How I wish it were yesterday." I looked at Tzion's appearance and was frightened. I saw a kind of frozen reflection in front of me. It had eyes without an inner shine, just a black sadness that grew with time.

My mother arrived, and I gave her instructions about how to run the house. But she didn't need instructions; she knew our house well. "Don't worry about the children," she told me.

My father, as if he saw what lay ahead, accompanied me everywhere. Wherever I went, he came with me. Why, Abba? I'm a big girl now. But to him, I was still his little girl.

During these days, my mother-in-law, of blessed memory, was

in a convalescent home recovering from an operation. We did all we could to give her no inkling of what was going on with Tzion, but she was too smart for us. "Why is it that you all come to visit me, and only my son Tzion doesn't come?"

My righteous mother-in-law couldn't be fooled with our excuses.

Then she dreamed one night that her beloved son was taking wing and saying, "Mother! I want to say good-bye!"

The next night she dreamed that her deceased brother — who had passed away several years before — was walking around enwrapped in a *tallit*. He told her, "I'm going to pray for Tzion."

So she left her convalescence to go to Tzion. But before she came, she went to the Kotel, early in the morning. There she found our children giving *tzedakah* and praying. Then she knew it all.

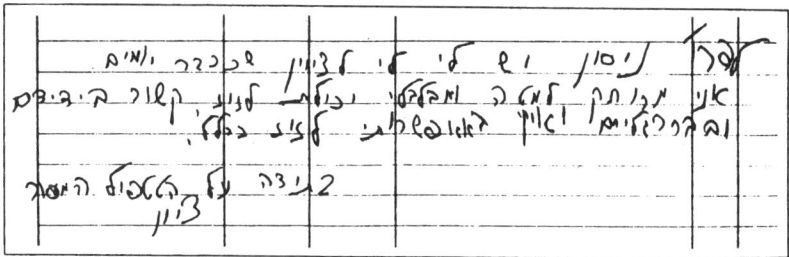

"Prof. Nissan, I have to mention that for two days already I can't move from the bed, my hands and legs are tied down, and I am unable to move at all. Thank you for your devoted care. Tzion."

The Heavenly judgment was in process. Tzion's condition worsened. He was bleeding incessantly. He couldn't be prepared for an operation.

The nurses worked tirelessly.

They kept giving him blood transfusions, dozens of them. We asked all the *yeshivot* to be on call to donate blood that Shabbat. We made the rounds of all the shuls. He had a rare blood type, B+. We called in Professor Nissan from Afula.

Suddenly, on Friday morning, the situation became dire. Tzion asked to see the children.

How can I bring them in here? Ribono shel Olam! The scene here is so frightening. We brought the older girls. Their father held their hands and whispered to them for about forty minutes.

We didn't hear a thing; his voice was so weak, it seemed that only his lips moved. With his eyes, he asked them if everything was clear. My daughters nodded to their father, and their eyes filled with tears.

Another few hours passed. I lit the Shabbat candles. Two flames in a goldish-red hue flickered, signaling to each other "*Zachor ve-shamor* — remember and observe."

Outside, a radiant sunset spread over the heavens. I pressed against the giant window at Hadassah Hospital in Har HaTzofim, gazing at this view of Creation, dreaming about sunsets and sunrises. Suddenly my sister-in-law walked over and gently placed her hand on my arm.

"Professor Nissan wants us to get donations of twenty fresh pints of blood," she said.

We spread out to the public telephones, our pockets bulging with an untold number of telephone tokens. We had bought them in rolls of a hundred. The phones rang and yeshiva students began to stream out of the *yeshivot*.

Again I stood opposite the giant window. I saw them coming, this one by car and that one by foot. There were dozens of yeshiva students, some in black suits, some in chassidic frockcoats. Knitted and black *kippot*, Sephardim and Ashkenazim, Chassidim and Litvaks and Yemenites. They stood in a group, sticking out their arms one after the other to find out if they had the right blood type.

Why are you making it so difficult for us, Master of the World? Why?

Not only was his blood type rare, but the urgent need for it had to come up just as Shabbat came in! And the blood had to be fresh, too! Ribono shel Olam, why? Why didn't Professor Nissan realize this one hour earlier? Then there would have been no need for this *chillul Shabbat*.

With my mind bereft of noble thoughts, that's what I was thinking. But suddenly, an idea flashed into my head. I ran to Tzion.

"You should see what's going on outside," I told him.

"Look!" his hand movements indicated. "I haven't got a drop of blood left."

"Tzion! If you could only see the scene outside. I've never seen such a beautiful sight before. You know, HaKadosh Baruch Hu wants you to be given fresh blood for your operation, the blood of young yeshiva students. And look, from every kind of yeshiva — the Sephardic and Ashkenazic *yeshivot*, Yeshivat HaKotel and the Mirrer Yeshiva... You know why? Hashem knows that you love all of them and you care about *Klal Yisrael*. He wants you to have blood from all of them running through your veins. Do you hear?"

I continued in a rush of words, "And the unity of Jews takes precedence over Shabbat observance."

On the fifth floor, about sixty yeshiva students were standing with their arms extended. Here, the bags weren't marked with the stereotypes we usually affix to each other. No bag was labeled "pure Sephardic blood" or "100 percent Ashkenazi." Here, all donors were accepted.

As I thought this, I wept inwardly. How tawdry we are, how lacking in understanding, what fools we are when we stereotype people.

Who, living under the chastising rod of his Creator, would dare ask what kind of Jewish blood will flow in his veins?

7 Av 5744

THE OPERATION TOOK TEN HOURS. Four of the department's best surgeons, headed by Professor Nissan, sweated over our beloved.

Ten hours of deafening silence.

I deposited my burden in Your Hands, Ribono shel Olam! What else could I do?

At 4:00 P.M., the door opened. Professor Nissan stepped out, his face pale. Rav Manat, Tzion's *chavruta* and closest friend, and Dr. Tzion Meshullam, both of whom had hurried over that morning, were also with him. These dear friends, and others like them, hadn't forsaken us in our ordeal. I truly sensed how they were holding me up and infusing me with hope.

"Tzion's liver is like the ruins of Jerusalem!" Professor Nissan said in a low voice. "Whoever believes that Jerusalem will be rebuilt, can believe that Tzion's liver will be cured."

Professor Nissan, who was far from being religious, was suddenly speaking in such Jewish terms.

I went out of the room again. Tzion's liver is like the ruins of Jerusalem! The words buzzed in my ears.

I could clearly see the ruins of old Jerusalem outside the hospital's large windows. I now felt them deeply in my heart… the ruins of Jerusalem. Tzion! My husband, too, bears one of the names of Jerusalem. And all this had taken place in the month of Av.

I tried to quiet the flames that caught hold of my body. Shabbat! It's Shabbat today! Don't be sad on Shabbat! In the pocket of my dress, I found a small note. Tzion had written it on the first day he was hospitalized, after they had pushed the inflated nasal tube down his throat and he had cried out in pain.

> Sin comes to cleanse a person. When a child is dirty, the mother washes him. It's only for his own good, so he'll be clean. Even

if he screams that he doesn't want to take a shower.

Tzion had written that — no! — he had *commanded* it!
Sin comes to cleanse a person...

They've brought Tzion to a recovery room, I heard my brother say.

I didn't move from his bedside until he opened his eyes for the first time on Sunday afternoon. When he woke up, he whispered, "Bring me a Chumash, a Chumash."

They hadn't let him take his books into this room. I ran and looked for the Chumash with the large type.

"What's this? Who is this for?" Professor Nissan asked. "You people aren't normal!"

Tzion sunk into his slumber again. His lips were cracked. Instead of asking for water, he had asked for a Chumash. And this while he was hazy.

"Prof. Nissan said that he never saw anyone like the religious and the newly religious studying in yeshiva when it comes to giving blood, especially right before Shabbat."

The room next to the Intensive Care Unit was milling with people. Besides the family, friends from all over Jerusalem came to join us. Notes conveying love, encouragement, and support were sent to us. They were lovely, very lovely. Especially during this terrible time.

Erev Tishah b'Av 5744

A LONG DAY OF WATCHING, accompanied by unbearable dread. Several times, when those wonder machines didn't buzz on time, I felt a terrible pinch in my heart. All that time I looked at Tzion's face, waiting for an eyelid to move, to slightly flutter, to show me a sign of life. Waiting for a thread of kindness, for mercy from our blessed Creator.

And then, slowly, he began to wake up. Suction tubes draining off unnecessary fluids were stuck in his mouth.

He made a hand movement. Yes, you can write, I told him. And his face lit up. He wrote:

A little wine for Kiddush... lechem mishneh... sing something....

"Sing something? What should I sing?"

Shalom Aleichem...

I didn't understand.

He touched my dress, his eyes expressing wonder. I was still wearing Shabbat clothes. Since he had missed Shabbat, he thought Shabbat was just about to begin.

"No, Tzion! I'm sorry, it's not Shabbat now," I explained. "They operated on you on Shabbat, and you have been sleeping ever since."

What day is it today?

"Monday. In half an hour, the fast will begin. The fast of Tishah b'Av."

Tzion's face grew dark. He bit his lips and tears streamed from his eyes. He wrote,

"Eichah yashvah badad."

The opening words of the Megillah we read on Tishah b'Av.
I brought him a *Megillat Eichah*.
Ribono shel Olam! He is weeping Your destruction and I am weeping my destruction.

NOW WE AWAITED THE RESULTS of the operation.

We knew that only a miracle could save him. In every synagogue, prayers were requested and Rav Alshich *shlita* arranged for special *minyanim* to meet. A public fast was declared and *vatikin* prayers were held at the Kotel. During these prayers, they recited the *Seder Ta'anis* and *Avinu Malkeinu*, accompanied by shofar-blowing. I knew that everyone was at my side.

"Regards to everyone in the yeshiva, and thanks to each one. How I wish that I — or someone else — could give an abundance of good things in return to each of you."

The situation grew worse. Every second we were hanging between life and death.

What a contrast between Tzion's spirit and his body! Tzion always conveyed the message that he was in control. There were moments when *he* lifted *our* morale.

I'll never forget the ties that developed between the nurses, those wonderful nurses, and us. They were so concerned about me and the children. They tried to convey to me every so often, gently and carefully, that I mustn't put my hopes up, because cases like these never hold out. I understood them. I understood them very well. But every additional minute that we had him was a "net profit" for me.

Then that awful massive bleeding started again.

Professor Nissan tried to push off for as long as possible another operation since, they emphasized, his chances of waking up from it were negligible. But this time I thought, if he goes into a coma, at least he won't suffer anymore. I couldn't even entertain the thought of what it would mean to be a widow and to raise orphaned children. I wanted only one thing, that Tzion wouldn't suffer any more.

Finally, another ten-hour operation was performed. A team of doctors labored non-stop.

And the patient woke up!

What a wonderful smile appeared on his face. Despite all the metal and plastic devices, he hadn't lost his human inner beauty for a second. His special, spiritual glow seemed more pronounced as his suffering increased.

I will never forget that one time when he sank into depression. I didn't know how to encourage him. He hadn't tasted food, a fruit, or even a drop of juice in a long time. The only taste his mouth had had was that of blood. I ran home and found a bottle of perfume, which I put into a bag along with some moist towelettes to refresh his face, and one of the aunts added some fragrant Yemenite basil from the garden to place on his night table. I was thrilled to have found a way of stimulating his senses to lift him out of his depression.

Bubbling over with excitement, I entered Tzion's room. There was a bandage on his forehead, and so many tubes sticking out of his mouth… my enthusiasm was instantly deflated. I left the room ashamed and aching for home, with all the items still piled together in my bag.

The only thing that couldn't be extinguished was the eye contact between us.

His eyes spoke. I thank Hashem so much that He at least left them intact. The memory of those eyes still lights my way to this day.

I AM LOOKING THROUGH THE dozens of notes he wrote:
- I feel as if needles are piercing me. Things are getting worse, not better...
- How I wish I could close my eyes.
- Will I choke in the night?
- The tube is deep inside my palate.
- I'm a Yekke.
- I don't want to miss praying Minchah.
- It's hard to breathe.
- Tell them to reduce the dosage.
- Three doctors made holes in my neck — for symmetry?
- Ask them if I can sit in the fresh air for half an hour.

Tzion was involved in his treatment and the medications they gave him. He showed such understanding of the treatment that one of the doctors thought he had studied medicine.

Tzion felt a need to thank the nurses. He wrote to one of them,

You are always great.

When I once commented on something one of them was doing, he wrote me,

One must know to whom one can make comments.

Despite his state, he was alert to the things going on around him. He wrote,

> I signed my signature for an urgent operation. Whom do we have to pay for the operation?

How can I not quote the letter in which he complained that his hands had been tied and he couldn't put on his tefillin?

A quote from the letter:
"I only want to cooperate. You assume that I don't understand a thing…. I am tied too tightly when it could be looser. I have to wash my hands, to put on tefillin. I am always willing to accept what you say, from A to Z. It would be a shame to ruin our relations toward the end… another two weeks. One of my worst problems is my inability to speak. Sometimes I ask for a certain thing, and instead, I am given Valium."

It happened when his health had deteriorated so much that they were concerned he might disconnect himself from the machines. But after Professor Nissan read his letter, he instructed the nurses to untie him.

How was he able to keep all the Torah's laws so meticulously while hospitalized in the Intensive Care Unit?

Later, when I was alone after the Shivah, crying over the splendor I had lost, I tried to understand.

FOR SEVERAL DAYS, TZION SEEMED to be recovering from the operation. HaRav Alshich *shlita* came to visit on Friday. That day was a holiday for us, since Professor Nissan had for the first time permitted removing the nasal tube.

We took advantage of the special occasion to ask if our children could finally come. My nine-year-old son hadn't seen his father for a month. He entered the room cautiously, and his father stuck out his hand to say hello. Suddenly, my son asked to leave. He was very frightened. In choking tones, he said, "Imma! I want to say *Tehillim* so Abba won't look so yellow."

He sat down and recited *Tehillim* in the waiting room for two hours. Suddenly, he stood up and said, "Imma, I'm going home! I'm going to look for a picture of Abba and I'll ask Hashem to make Abba look like the picture again."

When Rav Alshich arrived, Tzion asked if he could sit up. He was so close to this righteous Rav that anytime he happened to be in his neighborhood he would pop in to get a blessing. And now, the *tzaddik* himself had come to visit him! How could he receive him lying down?

Look what joy can do for a sick person. Tzion, who couldn't even speak, wrote in honor of the Rav:

"Baruch Hashem, Who has not ceased dealing kindly with me nor put an end to His kindnesses. Every day, you see His wonders. I also heard the voices of all the people outside praying, both young and old. I cannot stop thanking all those who are doing and enabling others to do this great thing. May they be blessed with everything good."

So he enjoyed a short pause from his suffering.

But as twilight approached, and Shabbat spread its wings, his health began to plummet.

Rav Manat arrived by foot, as usual.

This time, more attentive than usual to the footsteps of death, I waited outside the room. Please God! Just not this!

❧ ❧ ❧

On Wednesday afternoon, secret information passed between the doctors that only a few hours remained. Rav Manat arrived at just the right time — like in the fairy tales. He recited *Viduy* with Tzion twice. But before he recited *Viduy*, Tzion requested, "Please, take me out of here!"

"It's not possible," Rav Manat answered. "I can't."

"But I want to take the child!"

"I can't."

So Tzion said, "You take the child. You take him."

I never learned what he'd meant by that.

❧ ❧ ❧

I didn't hear the doctors' whispered messages wafting between the walls. I thought there was still time. Why didn't I know... or maybe in this difficult hour, I was refusing to see the truth?

I permitted myself to go home during the last watch of the night to change my clothes, to lay my head on a pillow in a clean bedroom, to wash my face, to give my sleeping children a kiss...

At 5:30 A.M. a knock came on the doors of my heart. "Hurry!" said a voice within me.

I ordered a taxi.

I found Professor Nissan pacing back and forth in the hospital lobby.

"Where have you been? They are looking for you. Quick! Maybe you'll be able to hear a few words..."

Quick?

I froze in my place. My feet, which had hurried so much in the last year, suddenly turned into heavy marble blocks. I stood outside the door of the Intensive Care Unit, finding it difficult to grasp what was taking place. If you don't hurry now, you'll regret it your whole life, I told myself.

Parting words are not a minor thing.

I pushed the door open. He was lying on the bed, his face peaceful and expansive, staring at the ceiling.

"Do you know who I am?" I asked.

"Yes, it's you — Brachah," he whispered.

Now, all the machines which had prevented us from speaking freely were removed.

He extended his hand to me, and I held it. The hand was swollen and warm.

"Why didn't you arrive earlier? I've been waiting for you all this time. You know I have to go."

He kept his eyes riveted on the ceiling all this time.

"Where are you going?"

"There! Look, right up there! Don't you hear how they're singing? You don't see how beautifully they're singing? Look! They're dressed so nicely... How can I go there wearing only a sheet — run and bring me my Shabbat clothes. A shirt and a suit."

I gathered the edge of his sheet and pressed it hard in the palm of his hand. I knew he couldn't see it.

"Here are your Shabbat clothes."

He felt the sheet and said, *"Thanks. Now I can go. Now I can go."*

"Brachah — move away! You can hear the singing from over there. The women are over that way. You'll find Batya there. You can't stand here. Don't you see there are no women here?"

I stepped back. I stood by the wall and looked at his face. I had never seen him so peaceful-looking. I had seen my husband in the greatest moments of his life; when we had married, and when our children were born. But never had he looked so at peace as now.

He looked above devotedly, and it appeared that he was accompanying their song, the song of the angels. The peacefulness began to steal into my heart too. I held with all my strength onto the walls of the room, but I felt I was tottering. My legs trembled. The compassionate nurses led me outside.

He went in his Shabbat clothes. They welcomed him with singing. What else could I ask for?

Each person's paradise is pictured in the light of his face.
(R' Nachman of Breslav)

The Soul's Glory

LOVE IS THE SOUL'S GLORY, being exalted in the glory of its joy in God, the radiance of its fear illuminating its grandeur. The light of its preciousness will then be found pleasing to its Creator in the love of its desire for the yearning for the lust of the Divine, to be crowned with the beauty of clean, pure thoughts. It will sigh in the grandeur of its ecstatic joy for its Beloved, the Exalted Beloved, and it will be bound up in the bond of His love and seek out and pursue the ascents to glow in the light of life. And when it rises and is magnified and aspires ever more to the knowledge of the holiness of its Creator and pulsates in belief toward its Creator, it spreads out in an excess of joy and expands in its happiness. It is then sanctified in the holiness of the Holy of Holies and is beloved and finds favor before the King of kings, the Holy One Blessed be He. At that time it is exalted and beautified and glorified in the glory of the majesty of the intensity of the glory of love. The Exalted One then selects it to radiate its splendor, to bring it into the chambers of light and bind it in the bond of life. May the Merciful One place us among the number of His servants who rejoice in Him.

(Orchot Tzaddikim — Sha'ar HaSimchah)

A SORT OF JOY PERVADED ME.

My sister-in-law Batya sat next to me. "What did he say to you?" she asked. I told her.

"He said the same things to me, but I was afraid to tell you," his older sister said.

Now I knew for sure that I wasn't dreaming. It was indisputably clear that this wonderful man had said good-bye to me in a state of holiness.

"I must get up and go," I said. But where?

My sister Ahuvah *a"h* (she died young a few years later) advised me to go to the grave of Rachel Immenu. Her friend from Beersheva, whose mother had died several months before, joined us. We traveled by bus.

I felt a special spirit accompanying me. The entire way, I sang the same song to myself, over and over, "If an army should encamp against me, my heart will not fear. I will trust in this" (*Tehillim* 27:3).

We returned in the afternoon. My Tzion had slowly sunk into a coma, and no one was allowed to enter. I knew that within a day or two, my personal status would change. And yet — even if a sharp sword is placed against your neck, don't give up hoping for mercy.

≈ ≈ ≈

How would I face them?

How does one speak to children aged nine, five, four, and in their teens? How does one raise a toddler without a father? "Ribono shel Olam, give me strength!" I said. "I have strength for everything, except facing them. You, Who grant wisdom to man, divulge to me how one speaks to an orphan."

At 12:00 noon, he suffered cardiac arrest. It was Thursday. The doctors tried to resuscitate him. Why? Why didn't they let him die peacefully?

I called my big daughters to come right away. They sat on the steps, their heads bent low, crying bitterly, "Oh, no!"

In the evening, I girded myself and went to tell the bitter news to my nine-year-old son. He was so close to his father. His father learned with him the Rambam, *mishnayot*, and the weekly Torah portion. His father would on occasion buy him a book and tell him, "Look, my son, if you learn it, I promise you that by your bar mitzvah, you'll have a bigger library than mine."

Abba — a father is endless love.

I decided to tell him the story about the corridor leading to the palace.

"Listen, my son," I told him, as we sat on a couch in my sister-in-law's apartment, "It is the way of the world that if a distinguished person, a Rav or a prince, comes to a palace to visit, he is received with great honor, and he is allowed past the guards quickly. But if, let's imagine, a stranger with muddy shoes knocks on the door, he is held back from entering. The guards ask him who he is and what he wants, they tell him to remove the mud from his shoes, and only then do they let him in.

"That's how This World is. Hashem sits in Heaven, and watches us every day and every hour. He looks us over and occasionally invites up a few guests. He brings the best and most important into the palace quickly, but the others, those who are still covered with mud, those who haven't cleaned themselves up yet and aren't ready to be guests, those whose actions are not yet what they should be, HaKadosh Baruch Hu gives them more time to examine and cleanse themselves."

I spoke to him slowly, using the words of a child.

"Why are you telling me these stories now? First you should tell me how Abba is doing! Does he still have jaundice and pneumonia? I want to know that instead of hearing these stories!"

"My son, you know that Abba is very sick..." The words choked in my throat. "Abba knows how to pray, right? We need Abba to pray for us now. We need Abba to pray for all of *Klal Yisrael*. We need Abba to stand near the Heavenly Throne, and pray hard that all the sufferings of the Jews will come to an end. Do you understand?"

"But why our Abba? Why can't it be someone else?" he asked.

"Because your father knows *Klal Yisrael* very well, and he loves them. You yourself saw how many guests and how many people came to him to get his advice. You saw that your father can be a good advocate for us. Right?"

"If Abba dies, who will invite guests for Shabbat? Who will support us? Who will build us a *sukkah*?" he said, with tears in his eyes. And with tears in his eyes he fell asleep.

Like a passing cloud,
A wind that blows,
Dust that flits,
He flies away like a dream...

AT 12:45 FRIDAY MORNING, 26 AV, Tzion passed away. He had the same pure, serene look on his face as he had had on Wednesday.

Good-bye, our beloved.

The Intensive Care Unit was packed with the medical staff who had spent the entire night with him, and with family members from all over.

It was then that I eulogized him. It was as if I had a recording inside of me which was talking non-stop. An entire year I had accompanied him in his struggle for every second. There were great moments of intensity and moments of weakness. At times I had spoken, and at times I had remained silent. And now, I could testify that despite Tzion's physical weakness, his spirit had not broken. The strong spirit that had drawn its power from Scriptures. He went on 26 Av – אב ו״כ, which spells out *ko'ev* — painful. In this month, all the Scriptures decreed mourning.

And from then on, I have gone on with life — but not alone!

At 9:00 A.M., Tzion's coffin was taken from the hospital to the *taharah* room. At that very second, the seismograph in Jerusalem registered an earthquake. Hadn't our Sages said that when the righteous pass away, the earth quakes? From there, the father of my children was brought to the courtyard in front of our synagogue. On this very spot he used to stand every day, stopping people and getting them to come inside and join the minyan. A synagogue may not close down for even one day, he would say. Because of him, not only was there a daily minyan for *Shacharit*, but also for Minchah and Ma'ariv!

His father, HaRav HaGaon Chaim Chubara, *ztvk"l*, had founded the Anaf HaChaim synagogue, and had taught Torah there with such humility. He was a unique and original man, well versed in all aspects of the Torah, a true light to the Yemenite community. Many years ago, his coffin had been carried from this place too. He also had passed away on erev Shabbat Kodesh. It was as if father and son had completed the same cycle. Both had left three sons and three daughters. How extraordinary! Tzion *z"l*, who had been orphaned young, frequently spoke about his father: "Abba would do it this way." "Abba used to say it like this." "Abba would have liked it this way." A link carried on through the generations.

Hundreds, perhaps thousands, stood in silence. From all over the country, people came and shook with emotion. We heard the eulogies, but my ears absorbed very little. My heart was focused on my children.

Suddenly, we heard a sharp wailing, "*Abba!*"

My son shrieked this word seven times when he saw the fearful sight. "*Abba! Abba! Abba! Abba! Abba! Abba! Abba!*" And then he collapsed.

"Abba" — how much universal anguish there is in this word.

I was about to run to him and tell him, "My precious one! We still have a Father! A very great Father!" but his good uncles gently carried him to one of their homes to get some rest.

With shaking knees, I accompanied my cherished husband. What a noble man! What a prince! My God in Heaven, I am placing a *sefer Torah* for safe-keeping with You. Now You have this *sefer Torah*. But what about me? Who will teach my children Torah? This solitary question lodged itself in my head and chafed. This question deprives me of my serenity to this day.

※ ※ ※

What a special love he had for Torah. He lived Torah. He lived it with his 248 limbs and 365 sinews. Tzion was a walking *sefer Torah*. He learned Torah in the Chevron Yeshiva and in the Great Metivta of Rabbinical Law run by HaRav HaGaon Ovadya Yosef *shlita*. Afterwards, he gained other wisdom, studying physics and optics in Machon Lev, while not compromising on his Torah study for even one day. He didn't want to get a degree. "A degree will just make me arrogant," he said. He only wanted to acquire wisdom.

One day, when trying to explain something wondrous about nature to me, he said, "You know, the more I study, the more I feel I know nothing. Everything I learn draws me closer to our Creator, may He be blessed. I feel His existence in the universe more intensely. It's impossible not to love our Creator. It's just impossible. I don't understand," he continued, "how scientists don't become *yerei Hashem*. It's impossible to explain the wisdom of nature without believing in Hashem."

To make a living, he worked the least amount of time he could as a *sofer Stam*, to supplement my salary as a teacher. We didn't want to be rich; we were content with living a serene, modest life. Once he was offered a job in the field of optics. The wage offered to him was several times greater than the going market rate — a small investment of time with tremendous profit. But we asked ourselves, should he give up a holy job for a mundane one? We traveled to HaRav HaGaon Rav Chaim Greineman *shlita*, and after discussing it with him, the Rav decided, "You must remain in a holy calling!" We gave a sigh of relief, and scrapped the temptation.

    🍃   🍃   🍃

My two big girls walked to the gravesite beside me. They were always my two right hands; two wonderful girls whose affection for each other made them seem like twins. Bringing them up was as easy as caring for a plant. I knew that they would never abandon me.

Please, Hashem! Help me carry on with the children as my Tzion would have wanted. Please! Watch over them from Above! Don't cast us away!

My daughters' tears wet the clods of earth that covered their father. No! No! No!

    🍃   🍃   🍃

Dr. Tzion Meshullam, a close friend of my deceased husband, a precious person and a man with many charitable deeds to his name, showed up on Friday night and told me, "I beg of you to try to rest. At least this first night, I want you to take a Valium."

"Valium? Dr. Meshullam, what good would it do? You of all people know what I lost."

"I know; nothing can provide consolation. I also feel that I've suffered a great loss," he told me, his eyes flooded with tears. "But please, just one. One five-milligram pill."

"No, Dr. Meshullam!"

"Give it a try, come on."

"All right — only out of respect for you. Give me half a pill. That's all."

Half a Valium helped me relax, and I slept deeply that night.

At 5:00 A.M. I heard my son's wailing. *Abba! Abba! Abba! Abba! Abba! Abba! Abba!* His wailing tore through the seven Heavens. I saw lightning bolts flash in the sky. I ran in fright to my son's bed. But he wasn't even in the house. Of course — he was staying with his uncle and aunt.

It was his wailing from the funeral yesterday morning. It was still suspended between Heaven and earth, trying to enter. Now, it had finally pierced through and torn the seven Heavens.

Abba! A word that can tear the universe apart.

Every time I saw the grief in my children's eyes, that word echoed in my ears and tore the walls of my heart.

Abba!

I ALWAYS FELT HE WAS at my side. Whatever I did, and whatever I planned to do, I asked myself, "What would Tzion have wanted me to do?"

I divided myself into two, the former Brachah — sensitive, vacillating — and the latter Brachah — strong, supportive, encouraging. Today, I am twice as strong.

Every time the former Brachah was about to fall, I galvanized my newfound strength to help that frail woman.

I carried him with me always, in my heart. The eighteen years we spent together gave me the strength to carry on. On the very first day, upon returning from the funeral, I wrote:

I will slowly cry for you
Slowly
Like your calm steps
Like the trembling of your prayers
Like the tune you sang when you studied.

Throngs of people came during the Shivah, the seven days of mourning, to comfort us. They came from the furthest reaches of the country. There were people who came and, finding the house packed, tried again later, and even then couldn't wedge themselves in. Only on the third attempt were they able to get in. Our comfortable apartment wasn't big enough for all who came to console us. People had to stand and wait in the stairwell.

Who didn't come? From the most distinguished rabbis to the simplest people.

I'll never forget several who made my heart tremble — to this day.

Rav Kaifi, may he rest in peace.

Just the Pesach before, we were returning from Ashdod after a visit with Amichai, who had just become religious. Tzion suggested that we visit Rav Kaifi who lived in Har Tuv. We went in to visit the elderly rabbi. He was so frail that, in order to stand, he needed the assistance of two people. We received his blessings.

We never know whose turn will come.

This man whose health we had so worried about, suddenly sprouted wings and came to comfort me. I was dumbfounded to see this elderly figure convulsed with sobs. How did he reach us from far-off Har Tuv?

He wept, and gave me an envelope.

༄ ༄ ༄

Another scene which I'll never forget:

It was Esther, a giant of a woman.

This huge woman with weak legs (I never could understand how her thin legs could carry such a body) was always supported by two canes. Who brought you here, Esther?

The woman trembled, faltered, and almost toppled over. The canes in her hands fell to the floor. She came from afar, and she had climbed up the forty steps to comfort me.

She knew him only from the synagogue. There, from where she sat in the women's gallery, she would listen to his warm voice. She loved the way he prayed.

༄ ༄ ༄

Another one I won't forget:

Naomi Tuvi, a coworker. Together we taught in the Ma'alah school. She brought me a special story.

Naomi, a courageous woman, was widowed a year and a half before me. Her husband and my husband had studied together in the same elementary school in their childhood. She told me a wonderful thing:

"At dawn on Friday, I dreamt that my deceased husband was dressed in a white shirt and rushing somewhere.

"'Where are you rushing to?' I asked him.

"'To the *chuppah* of Tzion Chubara,' he replied.

"That's when I knew that you, too, were a widow."

༄ ༄ ༄

Nili Eisen also came. Her husband, Dov, was a good friend of my husband's from the Katamon neighborhood. Nili was trembling. "You should hear what happened to us!" she said. "On Friday morning, at 8:30, the mezuzah that Tzion wrote for us fell to the floor. I lifted it up and said, 'Oh no! Something for sure must have happened to Tzion!' No other mezuzah fell, just that one — and it was nailed firmly to the doorpost!"

I told her that something had broken at my house, too. On *motza'ei Shabbat*, two weeks before Tzion was hospitalized, we heard a mighty sound of something shattering immediately after midnight. We immediately searched for the cause of the noise, and to my shock, found that a small shelf in the living room — which had also been firmly nailed to the wall — had crashed to the floor. The pretty glazed flowerpot on it, which contained a plant I had received from a neighbor when we moved into our apartment several months earlier, had smashed to pieces.

The shards of the flowerpot, the crumbled dirt and the uprooted plant reminded me at that second of a human grave. I'll never know why I felt such a strong, concrete association. That entire week, I couldn't bring myself to go near the fragments and clean up the mess. Only on Friday, as Shabbat drew near, I forced myself with tears in my eyes to clean up the mess in honor of Shabbat.

Again and again, we examined the large screws which had held up the shelf and couldn't find any logical explanation for why the shelf had fallen.

The omens indicating the oncoming tragedy were blatant.

꙰ ꙰ ꙰

Among those who came to comfort us was a woman I didn't know.

"We don't know each other," she said. "I just came to tell you something."

"My son and your son go to the same nursery school. Several times I saw your husband coming to take your child. Other people come to the nursery school at the same time, but your husband always drew my attention because he was always so helpful to the children. He would button up their coats, carry their bags, and help them cross the street. He was never in a rush. Once I asked who he was, and when I saw the funeral announcement today, I decided to come and tell you this."

She told me what I already knew. He was always running. But when it came to a mitzvah, he knew how to take his time.

DURING THE SHIVAH, YOU SIT on a thin mattress on the floor. It was hot, being the month of Av.

And then it was Rosh Chodesh, the beginning of the month of Elul, the month of Heavenly mercy.

We sat Shivah, and the masses came. Each person had his burden and, sitting with us, found release for his own pain. I had no idea that there were so many widows! Suddenly, it seemed as if all of them had come to me. Among them were elderly women who had become widows in their twenties and had never remarried. They spoke with painful yearning about that period of their lives.

What do you want from us, Ribono shel Olam? Our understanding is so limited. You gave us senses to help us discern, but I am blind in the face of Your grand plans. Please open my eyes!

Every blessing, every verse quoted, every person's remark, every caring glance, had manifold impact. The meaning of life began to change for me. Life received an added dimension, new and more profound. I tried to sharpen my senses, to absorb it all, not to lose a drop. I wanted to learn and know more and more.

We sat Shivah — Tzion's mother, his sisters, my daughters, and I on one side of the room, and his brothers and my sons on the other. The rest of the relatives took care of the little ones, and when they wanted to come to us, they came and asked questions non-stop. It all seemed to them like a show.

"I don't like these people. Who are they? They keep patting me all day long!" my little daughter said sourly.

"I'll just wait for Abba. Every day I'm checking to see if he's come yet," my little son said.

❦   ❦   ❦

During the Shivah, you sit and absorb things, yet you can't absorb it all. The tape recorder was constantly running; my son insisted on recording all the stories.

Between Minchah and Ma'ariv, our custom is to chant elegies according to the order of the alphabet. I heard the voice of an elderly man chanting a special tune which recalled the destruction of the *Beit HaMikdash*:

"My beloved and my sweet one traveled away…
"I don't know where he went
"Oh, they have made me sit down enshrouded, for he was called to the house of the King…"

The rest of this elegy solicited mercy for the dead and the living.

❦   ❦   ❦

My father and mother *shlita* tended to me throughout it all. Quietly, without blinking an eye, between their tears, they did what had to be done. I knew they were keeping something from me. I didn't press them; I knew the day would come when they would tell me. And then, in the middle of the Shivah, they couldn't hold back any longer and they told me their secret.

A month before Tzion was hospitalized, both my parents dreamed the same dream on the same Shabbat night. There was a commotion in our house, and many people bustling around. It reminded them of Shivah. My father woke up frightened, fell asleep again, and again dreamed the same dream. This time he dreamed the verse, "The whole house of Yisrael shall weep about the conflagration" (*Vayikra* 10:6).

My father woke up again in a fright, tried to calm down, and again went to sleep. Again he dreamed the same verse.

My parents waited anxiously for the end of Shabbat, then phoned us up and asked how Tzion was doing. I answered that all was fine. Things were normal, *baruch Hashem*.

"How is Tzion feeling?" my father said in a smothered cry. Imma also cried. They continued probing.

Until that day I had hidden the truth from them. That Thursday the doctor had told us to fly immediately for an urgent operation in Georgia.

"Abba! How did you know that the situation was much more complicated than we admitted?" I pressed him.

"We felt it. Our senses told us," Abba said.

And now, during the Shivah, they gathered their courage and told us about the dream.

🖎 🖎 🖎

My sister-in-law Batya sat beside me, and she told me something amazing. She said that Tzion had told her about a dream he had had before he was hospitalized. The dream bothered him, and he had kept it from me, but when he felt that he could no longer conceal it, he told it to his older sister. He had dreamed that his father, Harav HaGaon R. Chaim Chubara *zt"l*, was dancing joyfully in our house. He had invited Tzion to dance with him.

Tzion knew that if one sees in a dream a deceased person who is happy, it's a bad sign.

Thirty days before he passed away, Heaven had informed him.

When I heard it, it reinforced my feeling that all is from Heaven. The tie between a man and his Creator is eternal and unchangeable.

*I lit a candle for you,
A ner neshamah.
A wax candle melts,
But you
Burn in my soul.
My candle, forever, like a Chumash,
Like a Chumash, on each tablet
Engraved in stone —
Like a Chumash, like a Chumash
In the mouth of a cheder boy.*

When Shivah Ends

THE DAYS OF SHIVAH ENDED. Now the real struggle would begin.

Before I could be the heroine who could answer the children's questions, before I could look straight into my older daughters' eyes, I had to be strong myself.

I began to search the rich literature of our Sages, of blessed memory, in books which my deceased husband had bought me in his very last year. He would occasionally ask, "*Nu*, did you read the book *Gesher HaChaim*? Did you read about the meaning of life? Read it with the girls. It's very important to know this."

I didn't realize that he felt his demise was so close.

I wanted to read about the depth of God's judgment, about the world of souls, about reward and punishment and the revival of the dead, all of it. I suddenly wanted to clarify things thoroughly. What is my role in This World? Why does Hashem buffet mankind so much? To what lengths does our Creator's mercy extend?

I kept telling myself to stay rational. "Do not take Your holy spirit from me," I begged my Creator.

Sometimes, I felt as if I were crossing a bridge over deep water, without support.

My yearning for my husband almost drove me mad. I wanted to know the purpose of this blow. He Who rolls away darkness to make way for dawn — can't He see my darkness? I asked myself time and again. He took the light from me because it was needed Above, I answered myself.

These days would pass, and then the real test would be facing the daily routine. It would tell me which is stronger — death or life.

Sometimes I found relief through writing. As soon as the holidays ended, I sat down to write poems.

When Shivah Ends

*Had you only seen, had you only seen
The eyes of tender Assaf —
Like your two mischievous eyes
Yet full of grief.*

*Had you only seen, had you only heard
Avichai's trembling Kaddish;
His voice like a lyre trembling
With elegies of mourning.*

*Had you only smelled the fragrance
Of two myrtles,
How songs of Messiah
Were in their mouths as if from myrtles.*

*Had you only counted among the rest
Your hidden tears;
Secretly poured out like water
Bearing their own pain.*

17 Cheshvan 5745

May A Tear Come Before You

*Would just one tear
Just one tear
Among the shivah
Kneel before You
And say thus:
"I was waiting for the days
To fill with a Gemara page;
That my father would enlighten my eyes
And fill my mouth with Torah."*

*Would just one tear
Just one tear
Among the shivah
Shriek its words before You:
"I was waiting for the days
When my good father would choose
A Torah scholar, a young man for me
To build a home with."*

*Would just one tear
Just one tear
Roll before You
And say thus:
"I was waiting for the days
In which my father would sweetly teach me,
In the Yemenite tune,
The Torah which was commanded eternally."*

*Would just one tear
Just one tear
Active before you*

Speak thus:
"I waited for the day
To learn alef-beit,
A schoolbag on my back, with a devoted father
And a smile to make a difference."

Would just one tear
Just one tear
Bowed down to you
Say silently:
"I yearned for the day
When my father would exult with me;
A time when the word 'Abba'
Would never depart from my mouth."

Would just one tear
Just one tear
Among the shivah
During a year
During every entire day;
The tear of an orphan and a widow,
The tear of a bereaved mother.

FRIDAY NIGHT.

We were not alone during the five Sabbaths of our first month of mourning. Rabbis and relatives spent them with us; they did not forsake us. But I knew the day would come when I would find myself alone.

Malaise threatened to overwhelm me. My nerves were fragile and taut. Every ring of the telephone alarmed me. Maybe it's Tzion, I would imagine. Every step I heard near my front door made me jump. Maybe it's him, I would think, staring at the door. Could it be? Perhaps it was all just a passing nightmare?

Just imagine for a second that he went away for a long stint of reserve duty... Yes! It's been so long... but the day will come when we'll meet again. What does it matter when? The important thing is that we'll meet again, I would try to convince my mourning soul.

One night I had a dream. In my sleep, I saw a young man from long ago, dressed in neatly pressed clothes and carrying a small case in his hand, standing with a shining face at the entrance to my room.

"Oh! I knew you would come! How wonderful that your reserve duty is finally over! I knew it!" I tried to get up, to go to him, and he said, "But I have to return, to go back there..."

He spoke, then floated away and disappeared.

I stood in silence next to the doorpost. Oh, Tzion!

A short time later, I would dream about him again. What a wonderful sight. A giant cloud spread through Heaven, a pristine white. My husband's likeness was sketched in the cloud. How huge it was! I looked again and again, and asked myself, why is it so big?

And then the cloud drifted away and vanished.

I dreamed of it during the day too. Oh, that cloud!

For years, I kept searching for him. So many years. On 22 Av 5749, I would write this poem:

In the glass cell
To sit and to look.
The world still pulsates.
A baby laughs —
A father's love,
A mother's smile.
Stretching forth a hand from the glass
To strengthen the heart cast aside
To search for you, my beloved,
Between a ripple and a cloud,
Between the tree and the branch;
Among winged birds.
To see you, my beloved,
Passing by me, flying off...

Yes. I felt enclosed in glass, locked up, seeing, but unable to sense.

That's exactly how it felt.

A WEEPING VOICE WOKE ME up. The cry of a baby. The sound of weeping, mixed with the beeping of a clock.

It was 5:00. The clock was beeping, waking him up to pray in the sunrise minyan. But the clock, of course, didn't know anything. It ran automatically: Tick tock, beep beep. No, I won't change the clock. Just as I won't change anything else. Everything will stay in its place, waiting for him to come home. The clock will continue to wake me, and remind me in the afternoon, too, that he has to go to Kollel... It will go on for years. What kind of clock is this, that never stops?

I left the baby for a second. Just to pop into the kitchen for a moment. It seems to me that I heard someone there... something...

I stand mute. I know there's nothing there. I try to choke back visions from days past. No! It wasn't that many days ago.

Look at this amazing sight:

It was 2:00 A.M., two weeks before Tzion was hospitalized. I got up to nurse the baby and noticed that Tzion wasn't sleeping in his bed. I saw him lying on the rug in the guestroom, with a Gemara and a flashlight next to him. A faint beam to cast light on the holy letters.

On tiptoe, I drew near to turn off the light. For a second it seemed to me that he was sleeping. He woke up and said, "I'm not sleeping, just nodding off. Let me learn."

"But you're sick! Go rest in bed, these are difficult days for you. Please!"

"No! I have to learn! I must."

Every night for the next two weeks, his bed remained empty and his pajamas folded. He knew that he was going, and how could he go without being prepared?

THE FIRST FRIDAY NIGHT ALONE.

I had no strength to hold up my head. I stared down at the tablecloth as we sang *Shalom Aleichem* quietly, in sad, doleful voices.

Where? Where is that song we used to sing?

My hand shook and the wine spilled. The children looked at me sidewise, with eyes that were begging "Imma, be strong."

I will lift the cup of salvation…

Salvation, Hashem! Salvation!

༄ ༄ ༄

For many more years, the cup would still tremble in my hand. For many years, I would still be unaccustomed to it. Every Shabbat got harder. At the end of 5748, I would write this poem:

Oh, shameful cup of wine
How has your beauty dimmed!
Where is the light and the kingdom
Of my pulsing heart?
Oh, poor wizened cup
Opposite the flickering candle
Of Kiddush and Havdalah
Of a repeated Psalm
Oh my cup, my cup of grief
Of blood and tears.
How triumphant is your beauty
Only in dreams.

One can act during a Shabbat meal as one acts during a fast.
(Likutei Moharan 57:5)

I'LL NEVER FORGET THAT last Shabbat meal with Tzion.

Amichai and Shmulik, two *ba'alei teshuvah*, were with us. Shmulik was still a "guest" but Amichai was already like a member of the household.

As if sensing that this was our last Shabbat together, Tzion was very serious. Deep sadness emanated from his eyes as he sang *Shalom Aleichem*. His warm glance passed over us, one by one, and over again, never stopping. During those seconds, I'll never forget, I shared the anguished thoughts passing through his mind, but I prayed in the depths of my heart that all my fears would prove to be in vain.

Please Hashem, don't let the evil vanquish us, I begged.

More than ever before, we sat listening to his *divrei Torah* and to his lovely singing.

I'll never forget *Kah Ribon Olam*, the song with which he began the meal on Shabbat night, a hymn in praise of our Creator's greatness and holiness.

Were a man to live for a thousand years,
He couldn't calculate Your mighty deeds.

Tzion would explain these lyrics so beautifully and clearly to those he loved, to those who sought their way to their Creator: Although man is of minuscule size in comparison to the vast universe, he is still the crown of creation, for whom the whole world was made. How much dynamism the word "man" contains — when a human being is close to his Creator.

It was impossible to sit with him without being inspired. These friends loved coming to us so much, and they came all the time.

Amichai, as if sensing that time was running out, came this time with dozens of questions. Tzion, successfully hiding his frail state, got up and pulled out *sefarim* after every question. Scripture had all the answers. As Tzion started leafing through the holy books, each *sefer* seemed to open as if by itself to the passage he was searching for.

This amazing thing happened over and over again that Shabbat night, and I couldn't help but call out, "What's going on here? How is it that the *sefarim* are opening up in this way?" A strange feeling had been haunting me all that evening, and the mysterious opening of the *sefarim* just added to my anxiety.

Tzion looked at me silently and didn't say a word. The eerie feeling stayed with me throughout that Shabbat.

Chanoch, a *ger tzedek*, came to us every Shabbat for the morning meal. Chanoch loved to pray in the same minyan as Tzion. This time, Chanoch, too, asked questions incessantly, and Tzion answered patiently.

Gradually, I noticed that a terrible pallor had spread over Tzion's face. I begged him to go and rest, but he said that he was going to give the class in the synagogue, as he had to finish teaching an important chapter in the Laws of Tishah b'Av. He walked out the door slowly, and returned half an hour later. Afterwards, I learned that he had felt very bad. He had apologized to the congregation and then left. Yaakov Cohen accompanied him and Tzion told him, "Yaakov! Promise me that you'll make sure the classes will continue! I can no longer go on with them."

I noticed an unusual tension spreading over his face when he came home. He lay down on his bed, and I wanted to do something to make him happy. So I ran to the baby's bed, disturbed his rest, and placed him in Tzion's arms.

"Look at how lucky you are! Just look at him! Look at what a sweet child you have."

He smiled, held him for several seconds, and then said, "I'm too weak. I can't hold him."

WOULD I HAVE ANY STRENGTH at all to carry on?

I pinched my leg every so often and ordered it to get up. "Get up, lazy thing, get up!" Afterwards, I slapped my arm and aroused it: "Get to work! One day you'll be able to rest forever! In the meantime, you have no time to waste."

I cried off and on.

My favorite job in the house was cleaning the windows. It wasn't the work itself, but the sense of release it gave me. I saw the sky blue of the heavens, the blossoms on the trees, the chirping of the birds... what a stark contrast between this lovely scene and how I felt.

And then, then I would ask the Master of the Palace, "Tell me, Ribono shel Olam, couldn't it have been otherwise?

"Couldn't You have left him with me for only another four years, so he could be at our first bar mitzvah?"

Or: "If You had left him... just until we found suitable matches for our daughters..."

Or: "If... if you had chosen me instead to be the sacrifice, and let him stay here..."

Ribono shel Olam, he surely would have completed the job better than I.

Tell me, Ribono shel Olam, was this really the right time to take him? Maybe You could give him back to me for just a little while, and then afterwards You can take him back again. What is he doing there anyway, Ribono shel Olam?

I would ask like a little child, and then bury my face in a handkerchief and break into weeping.

When does one leave off mourning?

There is no limit or fixed time. One weeps over eternal magnificence forever... forever.

I would close myself in the house and weep three or four hours each day. I couldn't calm myself down. Far from it.

I knew that it was forbidden to mourn excessively, and Heaven is critical of one who weeps too much. I knew that. But only the Ribono shel Olam understood me. Only He knew how connected we were.

Did we sense how short our time together would be? I don't know why, or what our hearts prophesied to us, but we tried to be together for all of life's experiences.

"One's wife is like his very self," *Chazal* tell us, "and he should honor her even more than he honors himself."

Almost every day we ate two or three of our meals together. If I hadn't managed to prepare a meal, then he prepared it. And it wouldn't be something he had just thrown together, either. No slap-dash job from Tzion! He felt it was a privilege to prepare a meal for his wife, just as it was a privilege to be served a meal. And he was never angry if a meal wasn't ready on time. He never complained about burnt food. He would react to such things with humor.

How can I not cry out?

Hundreds of stories testify to the telepathic connection between us. I'll bring just one example here which made the rounds in our family, because it was particularly interesting:

One Sunday afternoon, we had an exchange of words in which we misunderstood each other. There was tense irritation, and a strained silence. I hated that silence. Generally, when something like this happened, Tzion would hurry to the *beit midrash*, and afterwards would return relaxed. As if nothing had happened.

That day I decided that I would be the one who would leave to get some fresh air. I went to visit my sister, but I couldn't calm down. I didn't say a word, except to tell her I had to go because I was in a hurry.

I headed for Geulah, a religious neighborhood not far from the center of Jerusalem. I just had to break that tense silence. So I decided to prepare a surprise.

I went into a store that sold electrical appliances, and decided to buy a Kenwood mixer. "Which accessories do you want?" the clerk asked. I pointed to the mixer, the food processor, the juicer and the meat grinder. He packed it up and I ordered a taxi and left. I asked the taxi driver to honk when we arrived home.

Tzion heard the honking and ran outside to the taxi. When he saw the mixer, he laughed and said, "Come see what's waiting for you in the house."

On the table was standing a mixer, of the exact same model, with the same accessories.

"I just got here a few seconds ago!" he said.

Imagine! At the same time that I was buying the mixer in Geulah, he had gone to the center of town and bought me one at Kalish's. To make me happy, he said.

Tzion phoned Mrs. Kalish. What an interesting story, she said. "Usually, we don't give money back after we ring up a purchase in the register. But, after hearing a story like this, I can't say no."

A soul connection like this is not a trivial matter. I can't remember our ever going to sleep with anger still in our hearts toward each other. And to bear a grudge? God forbid. Tzion felt as if the *Shechinah* surrounded him. He wanted no part of ongoing dissension — if there's a quarrel, you work it out immediately! You don't make a long-term issue of it!

I'LL NEVER KNOW WHAT was transpiring in the hearts of my older daughters, because each person's heart is private. Each person has his own "combination lock." Of course we spoke about Abba. We mentioned him and spoke of him with yearning. No, we certainly weren't silent! But I noticed that silence surrounded my older girls. In contrast, my four- and five-year-old children didn't stop questioning and asking.

"Imma!" the little children asked right after the Shivah. "Imma! What is HaKadosh Baruch Hu made of? We thought it over," they confided in me, "and we decided He can't be made of wood, because a tree can be broken or burnt down. He can't be made of metal because metal can be twisted. Not from fabric either."

"I think," said my little daughter, "that He's made of air. Because you can see through air, and air is everywhere, right? But just tell me — does air have power? How does He have so much power? How did He have the power to overcome our Abba?"

Again I felt helpless, as I tried to explain that the Creator is not a body, nor has He any likeness to a body.

The children wanted a concrete explanation. When we went out for a walk, my four-year-old child said to me, "I've been thinking and thinking, and now I want to tell you a secret."

"What is it?" I asked.

"When I grow up, I want to be a great doctor with a private ambulance."

"How come?" I asked.

"So when you're sick, I can run to take care of you real fast. Then you won't die like Abba. The doctors couldn't take care of him."

I realized that a storm was raging in his heart. As if to prove it, I heard him singing a song that he composed while playing on the piano, and which I immediately wrote down.

I know that there are soldiers who are shot in a battle
   and don't die.
And I know that there are glasses that fall and don't break.
There are birds who are injured and can't fly but still
   don't die…

This four-year-old child wanted to ask: Why didn't You leave me at least a disabled father? Five years later, I would yet hear from his mouth the following question:

"Imma, when will I finish my mourning?"

"Mourning?" I asked. "What do you call mourning?"

"Imma, here" (he pointed to the center of his chest), "I feel I am always in mourning."

"When do you feel it?"

"Wherever I go, it comes with me. In the synagogue, at home, in the Talmud Torah… every where I feel my mourning," he said. "How much longer will I feel this?" he asked. I didn't know what to answer him

I tried to ease his pain and to shower him with love, as much as I could. We continued walking, running, and laughing. One day, as we left the zoo, after I had spent hours trying to give them a sensation of happiness, my daughter asked me, "Imma, can animals also become sad?"

THE EMPTY SPACE WHICH their father's loss left in my children's hearts will never be filled, but maybe, maybe, I thought, I can succeed in diminishing the pain, if even only a little. The questions about life and death, about the revival of the dead and Mashiach, kept coming non-stop. The children wouldn't give up. They wanted their father. Smart children need clear answers. If they're not given them, their pure souls may be adversely affected. One has to think this over carefully, to learn how to formulate answers that calm the soul.

So I sat down and studied Rav Tukochinsky's *Gesher HaChaim*, Section 3. This book helped me tremendously, and I recommend it to everyone. Tzion bought me this book several months before he passed away, asking me, "Sit down and study this with our older girls." At the time, I didn't understand why he kept repeating his request for us to learn the meaning of life.

He was giving me provisions for my way. Now I had to explain sublime and difficult concepts to little children. How does one do this?

One day I sat comfortably on the balcony and told my children,

"Darlings, I want to give you balloons, not for playing with but to learn something."

I gave a balloon to each child. Red, yellow, and blue. They blew up the balloons.

"What do the balloons all have in common?" I asked.

"They're all made of rubber."

"Good. What else?"

"They're all tied with a rubber band."

"Great! What else?"

"They can float in the air and burst!"

"I'm looking for something else. Something important that turns them into big balloons."

"Of course!" my five-year-old daughter said. "They have air inside. Without air, they wouldn't be balloons!"

"Terrific! Right, children, now — the most important thing is the air inside the balloon. All these balloons contain air. It's the most important thing they have in common.

"Now, what would happen if we pricked them?" I asked.

"They would burst."

"Right. Now let's leave the balloons aside for a minute. I want to tell you a very interesting story, and whoever listens all the way to the end will get a prize."

Ribono shel Olam! I thought in my heart. Look at the joy these children have looking at colored balloons. Give me the strength to help them keep this joy. Don't let me become confused, help me say these difficult things in the right words.

The balloons were put in a corner of the balcony.

"Okay," I began the story. "In the morning, we pray:

My God
The soul You gave me
Is pure.
You created it
You formed it
And You blew it into me
And You watch over it within me.
And one day You will take it from me
And will give it back to me in the future.

"Children, what is a soul?"

"A soul is something important," my daughter said.

"Abba's soul is in Heaven," someone else added.

"So now listen well. When HaKadosh Baruch Hu created the first man, what did He create him from?"

"From the earth."

"And then He blew a spirit of life into his nostrils, just as we blew air into the balloon. Hashem blew air into man. The air that HaKadosh Baruch Hu blew into us is called a soul. We also blew up balloons and put air into them, but the air we blew into them was just regular air.

"Our air is everywhere. Our good and merciful God created the world, and filled it with air all over, so it would be enough for the needs of all the people, animals, and birds in the world. We don't have to buy air, and it's available to both the rich and the poor. No one has to fight over it. If we burst the balloon, the balloon's air just goes out and mixes with all the other air in the world.

"But Hashem's air is special and precious — it's the soul. Hashem gives us a soul when we're born, and it's very precious and pure, and we have to guard it carefully."

The children were listening intently.

"Do you know why the soul is so precious and important?" I asked.

They looked at each other.

"Because," I added, "the soul has special powers which Hashem gave us. This power is called *Yesod*.

"And when a person passes away, the soul leaves the body and returns to the place where it came from, to Hashem."

"What happens to the body?" the children wanted to know.

This was it. Until now, I hadn't dared tell them where their father's final resting place was.

"Okay, listen well, my dear children. We learned that Hashem created the first man from the earth, the *adamah*, and that's why he was called 'Adam,' right? Do you know why he was created from earth, of all things?" I asked. "Because the earth has a very special and important power."

"Yes! The earth grows fruits for us!" the children cried.

"Right. If we didn't have the earth, where would the trees sprout? But the ground also has the power to guard the body after the soul leaves it. Therefore, when a person dies, they put him into the ground."

The children looked at each other stunned.

"So when will Abba come back?" my son asked.

"If you listen well, you'll understand when Abba will return," I replied.

"Okay, so HaKadosh Baruch Hu is watching a *tzaddik*'s body carefully in the ground, and the *tzaddik*'s soul He watches carefully in Heaven."

"Where in Heaven?"

"In a very important place. Under the Throne of Glory."

"Who sits on that Throne of Glory?"

"HaKadosh Baruch Hu, Who created the world and is very great. He sits on the Throne of Glory."

"And when Abba gets tired, does Hashem let him sit on the Throne of Glory?"

"In Heaven, the souls are never tired. They're happy."

"What are they happy about?"

"They're happy because they see us keeping mitzvot. Every time we recite a blessing or pray nicely, Abba's soul is happy and is filled with lots of strength.

"So when will Abba come back?"

"When Hashem gives the order for the soul to return to the body. Then there will be the Revival of the Dead, and all the *tzaddikim* will come back."

"How could that be!" my little daughter giggled.

"I'll explain that to you tomorrow, *im yirtzeh Hashem*."

WE STARTED THE NEXT DAY by playing with balloons. During the game, two balloons burst.

"Can we tape something on the balloon to fix it?" my daughter asked.

"Some things can be fixed with tape. You can put tape on a balloon but the air will still slowly fizzle out. It's very difficult to fix a balloon with tape. But, one can certainly make a new balloon from the remnants of the old balloon. If we take the burst balloon to a factory, they can use the rubber of the burst balloon to make a new balloon. Let's go back to our story from yesterday."

I had carefully prepared several days ago for today's discussion. I had taken beans and placed them in wet cotton. I suggested to my children that we grow a new bean plant. We had watched the beans for several days, and had discovered to our surprise that some of the beans had split in two, shoots emerging from them. The shoots grew and became slender green stems.

"Look at the beans now, children! What happened to them?"

The children quickly perceived that the original beans had rotted, and new sprouts were growing out of them. We would shortly have real plants growing.

"Now, children, let's decide. What's better — to keep the bean plants growing in the cotton, or to plant them in the ground?"

The children were excited by the question. They suggested that it was better to plant them in the ground.

"Yes — if we plant them in the ground, the bean plants will get more strength than they can get from just cotton and water, and they'll grow better. Now, what did we learn yesterday?"

"That the ground is very powerful."

"Right, now pay attention, dear children. Our beans were dry and white and hard like all beans in a bag or jar, right? But what happened when we put them in water? They rotted, and *after they rotted*, a new plant sprouted from each one!"

"That happens to all plants?" the children asked in amazement.
"Yes."

To further demonstrate this, I took several beautiful apples. We opened the apples and discovered tiny seeds inside.

"Okay, kids, if we want to grow an apple tree, what do we do?"

"We take this little seed and plant it, and then a tree will grow."

"Right, because inside this tiny seed are all the important things needed to grow a huge apple tree. If we put it in the ground and pray to our good Hashem to send down rain, and if we continue to pray that the sun will come out every day to warm the tree, then a huge tree full of apples will grow."

"How nice!" the children marveled.

"Now pay attention! Every day we see wonders like these, great wonders, all of which Hashem created. He loves us and He made these lovely things in our honor. And we love Hashem too, right?"

"Not so much!" my daughter said. "He took Abba from us!"

We went for a walk. On our way, we stopped next to fruit trees and non-fruit trees, and we spoke about the differences between them. Afterwards, I sat down, tired, on a bench in the park, and they had a good time on the slides. I decided to put off the main thing I wanted to say for tomorrow. Maybe the stories I told them would seep slowly into their little hearts.

THE NEXT DAY WE SAT down and remembered again the wonderful prayer we say in the morning:

My God
The soul You gave me
Is pure.
You created it
You formed it
And You blew it into me
And You watch over it within me.
And one day You will take it from me
And will give it back to me in the future.

"What did we already learn?" I asked.
"That we have a soul."
"Where is it from?"
"From the Ribono shel Olam."
"The soul is a very important gift."
"What else did we learn?"
"That a great apple tree sprouts from a little seed."

"Okay, now, HaKadosh Baruch Hu is the Father of the entire world. He created the world and He alone decides who will go down to live in it. He decides who will be a king, who will be rich, and who will be poor. Who will be wise and who will be foolish. Who will be strong and who will be weak. Hashem rules over all the countries. Only He decides which country will have peace and tranquility, and which country will, *chas v'shalom*, have war, because the whole world belongs to Hashem. But, with our good deeds and our prayers, we can ask Hashem to change a bad decree into a good one. He always helps us because He loves us.

"What do we say in the prayer? 'You watch over it within me.' Hashem watches over our soul in our body, and when He wants — He takes it to Himself. Just like yesterday, when we played with balloons and two of them burst. If we wanted to watch over them, we could have put them in the closet and they wouldn't have burst. The balloons are ours, and we decide whether to keep them or to let them burst.

"That's what happened with Abba's precious soul. Right now it's being watched over carefully by Hashem. And when Hashem wants, He'll give the soul an order and He'll tell it, 'Now return to your body.' All the *tzaddikim* will then return to their bodies, just like the bean seeds which sprouted new bean plants.

"This special power to create something anew is Hashem's alone. Only He decides when it will be. We're careful to return the body to the ground, because man was made from earth. That's why we put a person's body back whole, so that the body's basic materials will all be there.

"But when will this happen?" the children asked.

"Dear children, this is a hidden secret, a great secret. But we don't have to worry when it will happen, just like we don't have to worry about the sun shining. The good and merciful God is able to bring out the sun every day. Just imagine if tomorrow, God forbid, the sun wouldn't shine, and if the same thing happened the next day and the day after that! What would happen then?"

"You can switch on a light," the children said.

"True, you can switch on a light to see, but you know that the sun warms the entire world, and only because of the sun's shining can the ground give its strength and do the plants have light and warmth. How else would plants get light and warmth?

"If, God forbid, it were dark all the time, we would be very cold, and might even die of cold.

"So therefore, just as we believe that HaKadosh Baruch Hu loves us and sends us the sun — and also sends down rain, and makes sure we have enough air to breathe and water to drink, and food to eat — so we have to believe with complete faith that we have inside of us a holy soul. And we'll keep praying to Hashem to hurry and bring us His Mashiach, too."

After that, they hardly came to me any more with questions

about the Creator's power and greatness. A kind of silent resignation stole into the children's hearts. Every so often I heard additional questions, and I also saw sorrow. But that tremendous, burning curiosity about how and why, finally dwindled off.

More than once I thought about how much strength, persistence, and curiosity little ones have. They force us to listen to them, and don't let us push them aside with meaningless answers. I learned from this that if we adults would keep questioning with similar determination, we would surely get further along in life. This inclination is rooted deep in our souls from infancy, but the mad chase after futilities dulls our senses, making us believe that the fundamentals of life are the trivialities.

One of the ways I tried to form a healthy connection with the children was through discussions. I engaged in many of them, perhaps because I was concerned lest, God forbid, I should lose the reins and the "horses" would gallop on uncontrolled. Nevertheless, it was clear that things didn't only depend on me. It was obvious that every child was capable of being willful, and could interpret things in any way he wanted. And so I prayed that I wouldn't stumble.

> *The "luz" bone*
> *In the spine of a man*
> *Which remains after the body degenerates —*
> *From this the body's frame will be renewed*
> *At the Revival of the Dead.*
> *(Likutei Moharan)*

MOST OF MY TIME WITH THE baby was during the morning hours. I would stroke his head and sing him songs. Inevitably, I sang sad songs. But I knew better. I mustn't project sorrow to him. Sometimes I played music cassettes with happy tunes for him. His childish laughter rang out as he heard each song. What would I tell him as he grew older?

"Don't worry!" everyone said. "He'll certainly take it much easier than the others, since he doesn't even remember his father. He won't feel the difference."

Time would tell.

Only a short time passed, and time told me.

It happened one bright day, after he had grown into a toddler and began going to a nursery school. He was only twenty months old, but he had already learned how life goes. He noticed one afternoon that almost every day a large man would come for each child, and the child would run up to him and shout, "Abba!" And each child always had the same man coming to get him.

My toddler waited one or two days, thinking to himself, "When will my man come? When will I run to him and say 'Abba'?" His man just wasn't coming.

So what did this child do? He wasn't going to give up. When I arrived that day, like every other day, at the nursery school. I opened my arms wide toward him, and called out, "Who's coming to Imma?" But he saw me from a distance and ran away.

"No! Don't want!"

"What's the matter, my child?" I bravely tried to smile.

"I want Abba! Abba!"

The word landed on my ear like an explosion. This was the first time that this precious pearl had ever emerged from his mouth.

"Come to me!" I begged him. But he was stubborn. He tried to hide.

A little child's mouth saying "Abba." He had learned the word "Abba" in his own way, by cleverly noticing how the world runs. And what could I tell him? Ribono shel Olam, You gave him the intelligence to figure this out! So now You, Ribono shel Olam, give him the answer!

I hugged him and he fought me. "Don't want! Don't want!"

"Enough! Let's go! Come!"

I couldn't promise him an Abba.

Since it was a long way home from the nursery school, we took a public bus. I sat down, holding my little one in my arms. And suddenly —

"Abba! Here's Abba!" he called out to me, pulling on the sleeve of one of the men who was standing near us. "Here's Abba!"

The young man looked at us in surprise, uncomprehending. I was impatient to get off the bus. But the story didn't end there. It had only begun. The child continued to fight me. I had no strength. I wanted to run away! But to where? To where could I run away?

To You — "I thought to flee from You," King David had said.

With my last ounce of strength, I climbed the stairs to my apartment, my refuge. I put my beloved son down on the floor in his room. He began to race around the house. He opened every door, the bedroom and bathroom doors, the balcony doors, and each time he asked, "Abba?"

"Ooz Abba?" (Who is Abba?)

I stood mute next to his older sister, both of us looking at this terrible scene and feeling the blood drain from our bodies at each heart-wrenching question. Then he ran toward us and shrieked, "So ooz Abba? Oo?!"

I took him into my arms and went out onto the balcony.

"Abba went away, away. You see that big, beautiful Heaven? We have a very great Father in Heaven. Very great."

That's how the next few years would go. The child just wouldn't let up. He would project his father onto one figure after another. Once it was this uncle's turn, and another time it was that uncle's turn. Every time I showed him a picture of his father looking out at him, he would throw it aside and scream, "That's not my Abba!"

I didn't know how much the child was suffering until he began to interrogate me non-stop. It began this way:

He was four years old when I went walking with him in the street toward the end of Shabbat. We walked slowly down the slope of the road, talking together. Suddenly, a car passed by.

"Imma, did Shabbat go out?"

"No, not yet," I replied. "In just a little while, the stars will appear, and then Shabbat will go out."

"Imma! That man in the car doesn't keep Shabbat. He travels on Shabbat without making Havdalah. Do you know who he is?"

"No, I don't know him," I replied.

"I know who he is. He's our Abba who ran away from us. He ran away from us and now he's traveling on Shabbat!"

His words frightened me.

"I told you that Abba passed away!"

"No! Abba wasn't old! Abba didn't die. Only old people die."

How could I remove such a terrible thought from his heart? This miserable thought that his father had abandoned him could cause him unnecessary obsessions. What should I do?

I began to repeat again and again about how his father was very sick, and there was no medicine that could cure him, etc., etc.

One day he said another astounding thing.

"Imma, you said that Hashem is good and strong. So if He's so good, and if He had to take Abba, at least He should make us a new Abba!"

I knew I would never be able to fill the empty space which their father's passing had left in the children's hearts. I tried never to leave my children. They always found an open door and a mother at home. I tried to be happy, but it was impossible to escape the questions. Sending my youngest to kindergarten was another difficult struggle. The older he grew, the more stubbornly he insisted on staying home. He would run away from the bus and I would have to run after him.

One day he came home all tense. "Imma! What do you think? That only grownups have thoughts? That only Hashem has thoughts? I also have thoughts! For instance, I'm thinking right now that I want to throw a towel at you. So I'm going to throw it!" He took a towel and threw it.

Afterwards he asked, "What is our Creator like? Does He have tzitzit and a *kippah*? He doesn't have them, right? I don't want tzitzit and a *kippah* either!" He threw his tzitzit and *kippah* off in anger.

His brother asked the same thing when he was six years old, as he returned from the synagogue one Friday night.

"Imma! Who says that a child who doesn't have a father has to be religious? To be religious, you need a father to take you to the synagogue."

Then he threw the challah cover and his *kippah* off, and cried until he fell asleep. This scene repeated itself several times on Shabbat night until he finally calmed down.

The children used to inspect every adult's behavior toward them with great meticulousness and incredible sensitivity. It seemed to me that orphans have a special intuition that tells them who truly loves them and who doesn't.

The following story was amazing.

I would come up with all kinds of plans to persuade my young son to go to synagogue when he turned five years old. One Shabbat morning, when I was doing all I could to persuade him, I rose early for the *Shacharit* prayers, and we walked together to the synagogue.

"You're such a big, wonderful boy and you know how to read. You have a shiny new *siddur*, and you'll sit down in the synagogue and pray, all right?"

He stood in the entrance of the synagogue and glanced a few times from the men's prayer hall to me. Afterwards he said, "Imma! I looked carefully, but no one is waiting for me there."

That's what happened the first time. But in time, I found righteous and generous worshipers in the synagogue who would show him the right place in the prayer book, but once my son returned to me and said,

"Imma! The 'uncle' I usually sit next to didn't come today. So I came home."

"But you have other 'uncles' you could have sat next to!" I reminded him of several men who were there.

"Yes, I know, but they don't have warmth in their hearts like that uncle does."

Such a little child and he already had his own spiritual thermometer.

ONE OF THE HARDEST TRIALS for a family that has lost a father is that of earning a livelihood.

"Who will provide for you?" my nine-year-old son had asked me when I told him the heartbreaking news that he was now an orphan. This was his first question.

"Don't worry, son. HaKadosh Baruch Hu, Who provides for the entire world, from the greatest to the smallest, will provide for us."

"But how?"

"Hashem has many ways. Don't worry. Let's just pray as we should."

I tried to implant trust in the Creator into the hearts of my children. I tried to fortify myself in this area too. During the days of darkness when I felt my world collapsing, I sought points of light which would get me back on my feet. I knew that only relying on the Creator of the World would help me keep my balance. Only then would I be able to struggle for my physical existence. As long as my spiritual conviction wasn't steady and firm, I wouldn't be able to support myself and my family.

Every so often I would think back to my childhood, to things I saw in my parents' home when I was small, and which were etched in my heart. Those wonderful memories testify to true heroism and single-mindedness in devotedly serving Hashem.

I longed to see this unity in everything I had undergone throughout my life. It was impossible that the Cause of all causes bestowed on me such parents, in a certain place, at a certain time, without a good reason. I was certain that the reason for it was so I could draw strength in times of crisis.

The burden was heavy. I felt as if big sacks had been placed on my shoulders. After one restless night spent without peace of mind, I walked around the house. I passed from room to room to see the children. I patted one on the head; I pulled a blanket over another. I marveled at the tranquility in which these sweet ones were swaddled.

The sacks on my shoulders aren't that big, I comforted myself. I'll yet merit to smell sweet fragrances from these lovely flowers, and they'll grow up, God willing. Nevertheless, until then, how much intense and wearying toil awaits me? What will be? How will I be able to provide for all their needs?

And then, as in the music books, a symphony of life is played, a symphony that reminds me of my youth. Abba *shlita* woke up every morning at 2:30, at the beginning of the early morning watch. He got up and studied Torah with unfailing persistence.

Imma woke up after him and tiptoed out. She would knead dough, and soon the fragrance of pastries and fresh rolls would pervade the whole house. That wonderful smell welcomed us every morning. Out of her mouth came prayers sung with an angelic tune, and accompanied by tears that only Hashem could count. Imma sang beautifully, and knew how to compose tunes as well.

Does Hashem wait for prayers like these?

Afterwards, she dressed, and silently, on tiptoes, left the house and took the first bus to work. In the evening, she would return happy and content, bringing food for her children.

I'll never forget the time she told us about how difficult it was to make a living. When she arrived in the country, when they were yet living in a tin hut, a social worker came every week to look for Imma or Abba and find out if they needed bread. But Imma would hide from her because Abba absolutely refused to let her take a handout from someone else. He always said that one should get one's sustenance from the generous hand of the Creator.

I saw my father doing hard physical labor. He worked hard in an orphanage in Bnei Brak and received a minimal wage. One day, which I'll never forget, I saw a giant truck arrive and unload sacks of potatoes. Abba ran up, turned his back to the truck, and a sack was dumped on his shoulders.

"Abba! Is that what you're getting paid for?" I demanded.

"No," he answered me, "but you know, this man, the porter, is tired and exhausted from his work. I came to help him." And then he carefully explained to me the Torah's command, "When you see the donkey of your enemy crouching under its burden... help him." If there's a command to lift the burden from even your enemy's donkey, how much more so should you lift the burden of a Jew who keeps mitzvot.

And it wasn't just one or two sacks on his small shoulders, on my father's slender body. I finally realized that a sack carries the one who lifts it. The Torah of Israel is the Torah of life, and for my father, it was the joy of his life. I can draw strength from parents like these, I concluded.

It is the charge of the generations and the need of the hour.

ONE DAY MY YOUNGER BROTHER came to visit and he had some news.

"Look," he said, "we set up a fund to help provide for you. We have receipt books, people will give donations, and then, God willing, you'll have a fund to take care of you. You'll be free of the burden of supporting yourself. You have enough of a burden as it is."

My brother looked pleased and relaxed — trying to hide the storm raging inside of him.

This information fell upon my ears like a heavy hammer blow. I burst out shrieking, "What?! You have nothing better to do than make me dependent upon others? I want nothing to do with donations!"

I took from his hands the receipt books — which were fresh off the printing press — and told him, "Now you're going to tear these up! All of them! One by one! I don't want any money from donations. I have a Father in Heaven Who will take care of me!"

My brother heard me and wept. He tore up all the receipt books. And that was it.

Only then did I realize that I would never be able to handle being supported this way. I don't condemn it — on the contrary, for those who are capable of receiving their living this way, it's meritorious. It's a merit to know how to receive just as it's a merit to give. But I was concerned that I might be tempted to depend on people, and then in the end, my trust in God, upon Whom I wanted to lean, would be undermined. Trust should only be in the Creator of the World.

And then, in the night, I again went out onto the balcony. I spoke to the Creator of the World.

"Ribono shel Olam!" I told him. "You're testing me. I'll try to pass this test the best that I can. Although there are three partners who contributed to making each person who he is, You, the main One, are Above. You promised that you would encourage widows and orphans, so I beg of You! Give me the strength and the wisdom to procure my living honorably. Don't make me dependent on benefactors! Please, Ribono shel Olam!"

A short time later, we found a crate at the entrance to the house. What was in this crate? I approached it, and found all kinds of goodies inside. Sugar, tea, instant coffee, flour, snacks for the kids, and more.

"What's this?" the children asked. "Who put all these things here?"

"Children, some nice person wanted to give us a surprise. Only good things happen to us!"

After I sent the kids away, I called my brother-in-law. I knew that he had arranged for a crate from Yad Ezra. I told him, "This time I'll keep the crate, but please, tell them that I don't want any more crates by my door. They don't know that I have everything I need."

Then I burst into tears. No more crates appeared at my house.

*As the gazelle cries for springs of water,
so does my soul cry out to You, O God.
(Tehillim 42:2)*

*When a gazelle is thirsty, she digs a hole,
rubs her horns against it, and bellows.
Immediately, water rises up for her from the depths.
(Midrash Tanchuma 22:14)*

NEVERTHELESS, CAN TEARS CREATE COINS? Time would tell. I was $15,000 in debt from the previous year. I had to pay the electric bill, the phone bill, and a hefty property tax. What should I do? How was I to get out of this? I sold the car and went to the bank. I opened up previously closed savings accounts and paid the debts. Now I could sleep in peace, without debts, *baruch Hashem*. But what about the future? What should I do?

I could sew clothes at home for myself and the children. But food still costs money. After a year, I decided to change my place of residence. I put my apartment up for sale, and at the same time looked for an apartment in the Jerusalem neighborhood of Har Nof, which was brand new at the time. I was impressed with the stunning views that appeared in every direction one gazed, giving a pristine look to the place. I'll establish my place here, I decided. I accept that good things come with difficulty.

I went through plenty of anguish before I finally found a comfortable apartment that had a balcony with a nice view. I went through even more anguish until I found a serious buyer for my apartment. But at exactly the time which Heaven had decreed, everything worked out, and it was done. I found my efforts had succeeded, and *baruch Hashem* I made a good profit honorably.

There is great virtue to a conversation which a man holds with his Creator, for the standard prayers, supplications, and requests are long known to the destroyers and accusers, and they lay in ambush on the way, sometimes succeeding in sabotaging them before they reach the Throne of Glory.

It may be compared to a highway whose paths are known to murderers and thieves who lay in wait to rob the travelers. But one who chooses a new path that is still unknown will avoid the destroyers. Conversing with one's Creator is a new path and a new prayer, which a person initiates in his heart. Thus the accusers are not lurking there and a person can hide his prayer from them.

(Rabbi Nachman of Breslav)

MY HUGE LOSS HAD LEFT a deep hole in my soul. No — I wasn't sad! I was broken!

I wasn't sad, for I knew quite well that Tzion had gone to a place reserved for *tzaddikim*. Inside of me were ringing his last words to me, which accompanied me everywhere: "You don't hear how they're singing? I have to go there…"

God's butterflies are beautiful
Pristine pure
In white wings
In Gan Eden

An orchard from the Beginning, with a tree of life
And the full light of a joyous river
The tune
And the music
With the revelation of truth.

I knew that I was also approaching that day which no man can escape. Nevertheless, I thought, I surely have plenty of time until then. How will I fill the hole gaping inside of me?

That day, the day of departure from life, no longer frightened me. It was as clear to me as the sun, that as long as you leave well provided for, there is nothing fearful about death. I learned in the book *Gesher HaChaim* that death is like being born anew for eternal life, just like the birth of a baby from a womb in This World. The holy soul implanted in us remains the same; only its outer garment changes. I clearly understood that I had no reason to feel anguish that he had gone. He had gone in his Shabbat clothes. But what would I do with the hole that remained in my heart? What would fill it?

I poured out many tears before my Creator. And not just tears. Songs as well.

I began to fill the empty hole with songs. Songs that I learned, and songs that just burst out of me. An infinite number of songs. Sometimes I kept humming a song or Psalm for days. For instance, I found great comfort singing *Mizmor L'David*, the twenty-third Psalm: "Your rod and your staff, they comfort me." If I can find comfort in a rod, it is a support.

I no longer felt fear of the great and threatening future. I knew that the reins were not in my hand. The Father of the castle, Who is merciful and gracious, exists Above, and the reins are only in His hands. Who was I to worry about the future? For the children's sake? The children belong to the Creator, and they just happened to come down through me. He would worry about their future. I would try to educate, teach, and guide.

"For a thousand years in Your eyes are like a yesterday that has passed" (*Tehillim* 90:4). Do I remember what I did yesterday? Just a few things happened yesterday, and this is what a thousand years are in the Creator's eyes. If so, time has no measure. It is eternal. Time for me is what I did yesterday, which affects me today. I'll move on to the future with it.

Time is the meaning of my life.

Time is actions and thoughts. I'll stand up with them before my Creator on the day I'm called. I'll give a reckoning, and say, "You see, Ribono shel Olam, I tried, I exerted myself!" Or — God forbid — "I was negligent, I was full of self-pity, I had no strength!"

Time is short. There is none to spare. Every minute is precious.

IT'S VERY EASY TO FALTER. It's very easy to say, "I'm fed up." It's very easy, because one's heart has yearnings, sorrowful yearnings, whose ability to undermine is tremendous. Sorrowful yearnings and sweet yearnings.

> *Time is like a seesaw.*
> *I'm drawn again to his warm voice.*
> *The sweet voice that he poured forth*
> *in prayer, in song, and in speech.*

> *One can recognize*
> *In a man's voice*
> *His royalty*
> *Because each person*
> *Has his category of kingship*
> *Which can be discerned in his voice.*
> *No two voices are the same:*
> *One voice is strong,*
> *Another voice is weak.*
> *One voice roars like a lion,*
> *And one voice is quiet and thin.*
> *There is also a voice of pain from the earth,*
> *And a voice of weeping.*
> *(Likutei Moharan)*

My soul went out when he spoke.

I heard both the strength and the weakness in his voice — the strength, which draws from the nobility of the soul, a distillation of his humility and holiness.

Facing the scalpel and the stabbing injections, facing the tubes, stood his refined and noble spirit, and I wanted again and again to hear that voice asking:

"Can I pray Minchah?"

"When is sunset?"

"I have to wash my hands..."

The constant insistence on washing his hands and reciting blessings, despite the deterioration of his body.

His eagerness to put on tefillin every day, despite the bandages and the siphoning devices.

His stubborn faith conquered death.

What a beautiful thing.

I want to see that again.

Rav Aharon the Great of Karlin said: Sadness is not a sin and happiness is not a mitzvah. But, what sadness can bring a man to, no sin can bring him to. And what happiness can bring a man to, even a mitzvah can't bring him to.

The angel brought to my small room
His white garment.
And took with it all of my secrets,
My joys
And my hopes.

So I touched the floor of the house
And it was cold.

And I'm intoxicated.

AND THEN...

One day I found myself gripping the car wheel and racing wildly to Hadassah Ein Kerem hospital. I was speeding because I feared I would miss the encounter. I have to meet him now! Now!

And then the car slid off the road and plunged into the wadi. And there, there I saw him for a second, and that was it... I woke up.

A dream!

I woke up in a fright, trying to find him... running through the house and finally returning to my bed. So I dreamed about him again! The car was racing, and I plunged down. And again we met!

I couldn't sleep any more.

I knew that I would wither away this way.

If only I could fill the palm of my hand with these yearnings, and take them and hide them, somewhere far away... until... until I'd raised my children at least... because I mustn't falter.

But no! Those longings were so concrete, cast in iron and stamped in my heart. No! It was impossible to uproot them. There was no way.

What will be, Ribono shel Olam?

I didn't dare touch a steering wheel again. I stopped my driving lessons.

No! I won't drive, at least not at this stage. I know it's just one step between me and death. I have a responsibility. This was my deceased husband's legacy. A manifold responsibility, multiplied without measure.

Opposite the holy ark, in a synagogue in Har Nof, I stood and pleaded for my life and the life of my children. And then...

It was as if the letters moved toward me and entered through my eyes. Letters that would illuminate my way and which would open a window from which I could look out.

Shiviti Hashem l'negdi tamid — "I have set the Eternal before me always."

What had I done up until now?

Until now, I had carried the memory of my husband with me. I held it tightly.

Until now, I had spoken as if to him. I consulted with him; I thought and dreamed about him...

And now...

It was as if a different cry had reached my ears. Much stronger and more ancient. A thousand voices, from thousands of years!

"I have set the Eternal before me always."

I've been on my own for less than two years. Yet what about the *Shechinah*? For over two thousand years she has been alone, exiled from her home. She has been a widow for two thousand years! Who is praying for her? Who will help her arise? Who will return her to her mate?

Then and only then, I began to understand much more profound matters, the matters which our Sages illuminated for us: For one who loses his mate it is as if the *Beit HaMikdash* was destroyed for him. Now I could truly understand the destruction, the anguish, the need to tear one's garments! It was so clear! The *Beit HaMikdash* is destroyed and we feel whole? I understood much better why I was alone. And I knew that the destruction felt by an individual is on a small scale like the anguish of the *Shechinah*. Now I had much more in mind when I pleaded, "Return to Jerusalem Your city in mercy." Because I knew what destruction was.

*Everyone should build a sanctuary
in the chambers of his heart,
and prepare himself to be
a sanctuary for Hashem.*
(Malbim, Shemos 25:5)

I BELIEVE WITH PERFECT FAITH in the coming of the Mashiach. And even though he delays, nevertheless I will await him every day.

I await him. Yet how does one wait?

"If the Mashiach were to know that the Jewish people were waiting for him, he would come," the Chafetz Chaim said. What does this mean?

It means that we're not waiting for him. That's why he doesn't come. What a blow!

Does every person have to undergo, God forbid, a tragedy in order to learn how to wait for something? To wait in anticipation for the Mashiach to come, to really want it? Why? What's the matter with us? Why are we so dense concerning the most wonderful thing that could ever happen?

All around me, things continue to surge as usual, and joy is rarely felt. Everyone is running, rushing, jumping, trampling, driving themselves and others crazy. And I want to run into the center of the crowd and shout, "Please stop! One moment! Just one second! Please, think!"

But my voice is faint amidst the noise; it fizzles out somewhere in limbo, and disappears without an echo. My weak legs carry me home, to the diapers, to the baby bottle, to the sunny faces of my small children.

I fill myself up on the prayer of "awaiting him every day," and the ache of waiting. My heart feels so dried out, as if its surface were cracking — I want to quench my thirst again from my spring. Yes, my husband was like an endless water source for me, and every day I discovered a new wellspring. The fountain's water, even if it hits a rock, will fight its way up until it smoothes the jagged stone.

That's how his voice was. So majestic. His voice contained the sound of the sea, coming to cool a raging heart. His voice was like a warm breeze on my heart, over which an icy cold was taking hold.

Now I wanted to hear that same voice and to drink those quenching waters.

But instead, a chill wind of bereavement blew in, and a cloud of mourning sought to discharge its heavy load. The iron-jawed monster of loneliness surged out from the fog. Its blows beat like hammers in my head, and its teeth tore at my heart.

The lion's jaws are terrifying when it slashes at its prey. Just as terrifying is loneliness when it pounces to attack. My longing for my husband was overwhelming. What should I do?

In my mailbox, invitations to family affairs, engagements, bar mitzvahs, and weddings piled up. *Baruch Hashem*, each person had his own way of doing things. Those who like to celebrate in grand style, and those who like a quiet, private celebration. But I didn't want to celebrate with any of them.

My soul needed someone in whom I could silently identify the same grieving. When a holocaust comes, a person searches for a mirror, for someone with whom to take counsel, someone who knows.

Sometimes as I searched I would hit a wall, and sometimes, to my surprise, I found a mirror. I saw there were others just like me, still in shock at the void inside. Because only when that void gapes open does it appear so terrifying.

But when those terrors hit, as in those first days of widowhood, I hung on to his words, to that tune of his, *"Don't you see how they're singing? You know I have to go..."*

And like those garden beds which sprout their greenery at the advent of spring, doused in the morning dew, buds of hope blossomed in me again and I began to sing:

"Even though he delays, nevertheless I will await him every day..."

The words in your mouth were sweet
Like date honey
Butterflies
Flitted inside of me

Butterflies on Mount Carmel's flowers
When fire consumed it
Burning and painting the heavens.

In threads of purple
With lines of gold
With scarlet threads
Linen threads
Crimson threads
Of my razed palace.

WISDOM IS THE LIGHT of the soul.

I saw this in my mother, may she live and be well. She sat by my side, words speaking to my heart.

"Don't stay in the house," she suggested. "You need to go out and work a little. You really should. A change would do you good."

She's right, I thought to myself. It would be a good idea to go out and work a little. To clear my head, to get a change of air, to get energized!

But what job should I look for? Go back to teaching? If my mother only knew how much oxygen one needs in one's lungs to do that... I need that energy right here in the house, to raise my next generation...

I found myself walking around town almost every day, to look around at all the possibilities and think about what job I should look into. Should I sell art objects? Maybe jewelry? Then again, why should I sell? Maybe I should create something? Jewelry? I couldn't see myself working with metals, although I was captivated by the idea — to take hard material, soften it, and make out of it whatever I wanted... Wasn't I formed out of material too?

But this time, I was searching for something delicate that would speak to me and warm my heart.

I continued gazing at the display windows. Like a tree beaten by the fierce desert heat, I walked along the street. Every so often, I stopped. One day I was about to return home almost as soon as I had started out, when suddenly I saw the flowers.

As if they were waiting for me, they all opened up. I knew them from long ago, from when a group of little girls in a village used to run through the golden fields, through a colorful mélange of anemones, primroses, daisies, and tulips. Their eye-catching colors laughed at me from the display windows.

Suddenly, I felt my fire rekindled. Suddenly, the heaviness vanished, and words again rushed into my mouth. I asked the woman behind the counter:

"Are... are you looking for someone to arrange the flowers?"

"No! No thanks!" the lady answered emphatically. "I do my own flower arrangements."

I left feeling strange. On one hand, I felt as if I had changed my clothes — as if I had thrown off the dusk and wrapped myself in bright daylight. On the other hand, there seemed to be a strange indifference surrounding me, which didn't understand the soft whispers of my heart. How could that woman know what was transpiring in my soul?

But the light was shining in my heart, and it showed me blossoming flowers. "Don't give up," I whispered to myself. I wasn't too bashful to ask at the next store.

"Perhaps... perhaps you're looking for someone who can make flower arrangements?"

"Not really!" The lady said. Then she asked in curiosity, "Is this your profession?"

"No! Not at all! But it's my hobby." I kept on talking, trying to persuade her. "You know that people sometimes invest more in their hobby than they do in their profession, because they really love it."

"You have experience?" the lady asked.

"Um... a little," I stammered. "Ever since I was a little girl, I've been picking flowers and thistles in fields... I always feel lovely when I'm surrounded by flowers."

"But I have no money to pay you," the lady said.

"That doesn't matter... I'm not looking for money. I came in because I felt an inner urge... you know what I mean?"

And an amazing thing happened: This lovely lady gave me flowers, a vase, and a piece of florist's oasis. I began to work on a flower arrangement.

I will never, ever forget that moment! For that one moment, I feel tremendously indebted. At that one moment, all the world's pleasures crowded together and piled up, one on top of the other. My hands sweated and trembled with the thrill of it. How lovely! I whispered to myself. How perfectly lovely!

The dew-covered flowers opened their eyes to me again, and I no longer felt thrust aside in HaKadosh Baruch Hu's world. I'll continue to wait for him, and I'll receive him with flowers, I thought to myself. I'll await him every day, until he comes.

And then…
I opened my eyes
And as if
The sun sputtered all its light
From its eyes
And kissed me

It spit all its fire
To devour my grief
And just the warmth and softness remained
That which
I had known
From days of old.

When I arrived home, I felt as if the way had become shorter.

That very day, I tried to find out where one could buy dried flowers, since that year was *shemittah*. I thought to myself, if I am making flower arrangements, I may as well try to sell baskets of dried flowers in our neighborhood.

I spent several days looking into the idea. I quickly discovered that this pleasure would cost me a lot of money. I had to buy baskets, ceramic bowls, flowers, etc. But this didn't discourage me. One day I arrived at the entrance of our house in a taxi, and began to unload crates. The children opened their eyes in wonder…

"Imma! Are you sure you'll succeed?"

"Why did you buy so much stuff?"

"If I don't make a start," I told them, "If I don't make an opening like the eye of a needle, how will the enormous hall open up for me?"

A long way was still ahead of me.

🌿   🌿   🌿

What is more wonderful than being close to nature?

There was a large forest surrounding Har Nof. Sensing the fragrance of childhood and youthful enthusiasm, I walked around unrestrained in HaKadosh Baruch Hu's world. I came across a storm-beaten tree, which had to draw upon its roots to survive. Here and there I heard the whistling of the wind pouring out like a silent prayer.

I collected them in my soul: broken branches, peeled tree bark, and pinecones. The ideas rushed one after another, and my hands worked with alacrity. The baskets were ready, filling the shelves, on the floor, and in the closets... but what would I do with them? I had no store or salespeople!

> *Sometimes an idea passes through the mind*
> *like a soaring bird.*
> *One needs strength and intelligence*
> *to catch the bird.*
> *(Likutei Moharan 58)*

AND THEN, SALVATION FLOATED down. It came in the form of Rachel Bodenheimer, whose *chesed* precedes her wherever she goes, and who runs after it so as not to miss it, constantly, like water coursing down a river. She just happened to drop by one weekday.

"Look how lovely they are! They're so beautiful!" she encouraged me. "Look, can you prepare a hundred bouquets by next week?"

"A hundred bouquets! What do you need them for?"

"I'm planning to make an exhibition."

"You have nothing else to do?"

"It's my pleasure."

"Please! Stop going out of your way for me."

"Don't you understand? I'm doing it for myself."

Whoever didn't see Rachel at that moment wouldn't believe it. She was radiant with the light of *chesed*, a light of true beauty. An enormous light created by her incredible power of giving.

The following week rolled around, and Professor Bodenheimer himself — today the president of Machon Lev and Rachel's right hand — took the time to be on hand for the festive evening. All their children came home and, propelled by the power of *chesed*, moved furniture from the guest room, detached doors from closets, and built shelves for the exhibition. They took out their best tablecloths and spread them over tables. They baked cakes, prepared dishes, and warmed up the atmosphere with classical music. They even bought a roll of film to take pictures.

And, unbelievably, they made countless trips in their car to my house to collect the baskets, "so you won't have to bother looking for someone to transport the items," because the mitzvah was entirely theirs. And they did it so perfectly, so joyously. I will never forget this, never! From the strength of that *chesed*, I was emboldened to go a long way.

In the evening, people arrived, lots of people — friends of the

Bodenheimers. What a festive atmosphere, and plenty of compliments. No, not that the bouquets were all that nice (today, after years of experience, I realize that those bouquets were simple and rather paltry), but I felt that people had come and spent their time to strengthen me. And everyone bought. One thousand four hundred shekels jingled in my pocket. I was able to cover half my expenses.

Rachel's children wrapped the bouquets and decorated them with ribbons. They served cake and coffee. The serene music turned on a light, that light reserved in my heart for only the greatest moments, for moments of true giving.

Two weeks hadn't passed before Rachel Bodenheimer appeared again. Another exhibition, and this time in the ritzy Talbieh neighborhood, no less! Thank you so much, Rachel!

🌱   🌱   🌱

More than the money, I felt blessed by the opportunity to be creative. It was an outlet for me.

I could make flower arrangements at any hour of the day. I was thrilled that my work was at home, and that it depended on me and not me on it. That way, I didn't neglect my children, and they always found an open door.

Slowly, the children also became conscious of nature. They had fun making flower arrangements too, and we spent quality time together.

Thus Hashem arranged a job for me that brought me joy. Most of the people who came to our house to buy flowers told us about their happy occasions. We heard about a new baby that was born, or a *chatan* and *kallah* who had just become engaged. We shared their joy. And in this way, the children saw that HaKadosh Baruch Hu's kindness is continually renewing itself in the world.

ONE SUMMER DAY I WAS on my way somewhere with my youngest son. We stood in the shadow of a tree near the bus stop, waiting for the bus. Suddenly, my son's hand slipped out of mine and he ran away.

"Where are you going?" I called, running after him.

"Wait, Imma! Wait! I don't want to lose him! He'll run away from me again!" He kept running.

"Where are you going? The bus is coming any second! We've been waiting long enough."

Then he wrapped himself around me. "Look!" Not far from the traffic light, he lifted a finger and said, "Imma! Look there! Take a good look! Imma! That's him, I'm telling you!"

"Who?"

"Take a good look!" he pointed to a strange man. "You don't see? He's looks just like Abba's picture! It must be Abba! Hurry, before he crosses the street."

I looked. His profile did look a lot like my husband's picture. A black *kippah*, a black beard, glasses. I felt my innards surging just from the similarity. My tongue became stuck, and I could barely press my son to me while shaking my head No! No! No! But by that time, I already knew that words and explanations are useless to a child who never knew his father. I had to do something more concrete.

To my great sorrow, a fine and special woman, who had fought an illness for many years, passed away in our neighborhood. I decided to take my son to see the funeral. He was only six, but I felt I had no choice. We stood at a distance, and from that distance viewed all those who came. We also saw the children of that righteous woman.

I explained to my son, "Do you see? These children also lost their mother, and she is now returning to the place where she came from."

Later, with my arm around him tightly, we went to the cemetery. We saw hundreds of graves lying next to each other, silent in the cradling earth. The only sound was the soothing rustle of the trees, which refreshed our souls, which were almost bursting from their great burdens.

We stood there a few minutes. I read to him what was written on her monument, and then he asked me,

"Is this place safe enough?"

"Is it safe enough? What do you mean by 'safe'?"

"Is it safe enough so that no one will step on Abba's grave?"

Several days of bewilderment and questions passed, but after that, the child completely calmed down, as if he had finally accepted the judgment. Again his sweet mischievousness returned, which was a cure for every pain and ailment in a mother's heart.

Flowers, too
Shed tears of prayer
Dripping on my hand,
Mingled in the whiteness of my life
And in the blood of my clothes.

Flowers, too
Sometimes
Shed a straying tear
Flowing from the fountains of silence
Of the vast deeps,
Emerging from the clods of earth
Bearing balsam and fragrant lot,
For Lot's wife
Who didn't know
That a cry lasts for generations.

I COULD HAVE MADE FLOWER arrangements during the day, but I usually preferred to make them at night. I could then listen to the beauty of the world when it was transparent and clear, without seeing the dust or hearing the noise of motors. In the silence, I could quickly traverse long distances and linger in that faraway spot for a single, long moment. It was a kind of nestling sensation of warmth and softness, a feeling I had lost when my destiny had capsized. The feeling had returned to me and sprouted forth again, like fresh shoots in a desert newly watered and fertilized — a kind of trembling feeling that made everything else seem inconsequential, a feeling which left me with my hands outstretched, open, ready to receive. To receive yet a little more! I wanted to stretch myself like an elastic into and above time.

All at once, I could put aside the question that always haunted me: would my heart ever again be filled with that balm which turns bitter into sweet?

I laid my head on the familiar pillow, the pillow that had absorbed my groans, the pillow whose feathers were dead but breathing. It had absorbed and was soaked with my anguish. I sank into far-off, sweet slumber.

That grief
That touched the wings of the wind
That made the leaves of light fall in the autumn
That poured my thirst into the desert's young shoots

That grief
That closed off the walls of spring before me —
Chase it away!

Because I sought to touch
The lips of the sun
Which opened luminous windows
With infants' shrill cries
On my knees
A righteous new generation

Go away, wailing, go away!
Go and bathe
In the mountains' streams.

I TOOK MY CHILDREN TO the seashore. The immense sea, where land and Heaven touch, the living sea.

Yes, just like then… when I walked beside my beloved husband to gaze at the beauty of the sea, to unite with the act of creation and bless the wonderful universe.

Here by the sea, I saw the beginning of the world, in this huge, endless domain that touches only primal yearnings, yearnings detached from the turbulent commotion that rampages in the world, detached from coveting, envy, shame. It only yearns for the place from which it came. That is why the sea hasn't lost a drop since the day it was created, since it never sought to take from others. It only watered, quenched, gave, and became filled up with these kindnesses, before again pouring them out.

I loved its whisper and its foam. So alive, so alive!

I wanted to bequeath this lovely gift to my children one scorching day. I brought them here to feel the sensations of the beach, to touch the hems of its garments. We chose a beach empty of people; we wanted quiet. The children sat down and decided to build a palace. A great palace for a great king, attended by many princes and dukes.

"Maybe we should build a *Beit HaMikdash*?" my little one asked.

"No! That's impossible. The third *Beit HaMikdash* will never be destroyed. So here we're only going to build a palace."

"Let's build it and we won't destroy it," the little one insisted.

"We can't. We have to make sure it stays damp, so we have to keep dripping water on it. If not, the palace will get ruined. You see?"

"Why?"

"Because without water it will dry out and our big palace will crumble," the older one explained. "We have to keep it moist."

"We have to keep ourselves moist, too," I told myself, "nourished so the palace won't crumble."

I looked at myself. I, too, was made from crumbs of earth, from crumbs of sand, just like the sand palace. The palace of my body is a small sanctuary, I whispered again to myself. Without nourishment, the "moisture" that is my soul, it will all crumble!

The sun's orb waned in the sky and then sallied into an immense sunset. The sun sent tongues of fire to lick the buoyant waves. They flickered with a bronze shine and rolled off to some faraway destination. They dove into the depths and again rose up to the flames. I thought of the turning blade of the sword that guards the entrance to Gan Eden. This is a sea of fire, I said to myself. Who can pass through it?

I again looked at the frailty of my physical body, the palace of sand, and whispered a prayer:

Please guard my soul, the life-giving water of my body, so that it won't crumble away as though it had never been.

> *The sound of music comes from the birds.*
> *(Likutei Moharan 3)*

WE WOKE UP TO THE FLUTTERING sounds of spring. The songbirds flew among the branches of the poplar trees that surrounded our house, and reminded us again and again that the Master of the Castle hadn't left out a thing which could help arouse our hearts again, and fill them with sweet fragrances of creation, human endeavor, and joy.

"Imma! How long does a nightingale live?" my son asked me.

"How many years? As many as the times it managed to plant cheer in people's hearts," I said.

"That's your answer?"

"Remember when we said that the only way to measure time is by the actions we perform with it?"

"I don't understand."

"Listen again: Time cannot be measured. The clock is an invention made by people to help us manage our time, but more important is what we do with our time."

"What if I do nothing?"

"There is no such thing as a person doing nothing."

"Why?"

"Because even if you sit on your bed with your hands resting on your lap, your brain is still working, and so are your thoughts, your feelings... so you're not doing nothing. There's no such thing."

"I don't understand!"

"HaKadosh Baruch Hu created us with many elaborate organs, and we have to use them. Some of them we can see, like our ears and eyes, and others are hidden from us, like the heart and mind. They're like tools which we have to use correctly, just like a sailor has to carefully watch the movements of his compass if he wants to reach the shore. The mind and the heart don't stop, even if we're resting or sound asleep. They keep working."

"So how do we use them?"

"We have to learn how. We learn how from the holy Torah. It guides us on how to use these important tools of ours. Both when we're sad and when we're happy."

Afterwards I went to the kitchen to do dishes. My son sank into an armchair, deep in thought. After a while, he stood up and asked, "If a person wants to be happy, but he always feels sad inside here" —he pointed to his chest, and I saw tears dotting his eyes — "what should he do, Imma?"

"Listen to the voice of the nightingale. Go out on the balcony and see how the sun plays with the leaves. Look at the blue heavens, listen to the whistle of the wind — and you will feel good. I promise you, you'll even be able to sing.

"The world is great! Huge! Broad! It doesn't begin and end in this room or in that sad place you have in your heart."

"I think I'm beginning to understand, Imma."

I knew that I'd placed a great challenge on my son. Way, way too great.

"On Shabbat, we'll sit down and discuss it more," I promised him.

At that next opportunity I explained, "Look, a person is called a complete cosmos. A man's body — his arms, legs, heart, and head — is like a little town. The soul and spirit turn the city into a complete world. Imagine, my sweet children, that one day we were to get up and see houses and cars — but no sun, no air, no movement, no plants, no life! Everything is immobile! What would you feel?"

"We would feel it's a weird world," the children said.

"Right! A very weird world, just wood and stone and that's it! Without growth or movement! Can a world like this develop, grow, or expand?"

"No."

"That's why Hashem made a world that can grow. He gave trees warmth, water and air. He gave a person food and air so his body will grow and develop, but he also gave a lot of energy to the soul, including the power to think, study, and contemplate. This power helps the body grow and become strong! And to be happy! If a person will use these wonderful things, he will always remain healthy — because a person who is healthy in his soul is also healthy in his body."

"So how does one use this power of contemplation?" the children persisted. "How does one use his thoughts?"

We decided to go out for a walk. Before we went out, we decided upon a goal. We wouldn't just walk randomly; we would try to pay attention to the plants. (I suddenly realized that every time I wanted to explain sublime, weighty concepts to my children, I always turned to the world of plants.)

"Look at that tree. How did it begin to sprout? From the roots which were planted in the ground. This means that the head of the tree is really in the ground, because most of its nourishment is from the ground.

"Now look at a person. Where is a man's head? His head is above and his legs are below. A man's head is on top because his main nourishment is from Heaven. A man is connected to his Creator.

"And how is a man similar to a tree?

"A man and a tree both need to be cared for daily, to be watered, and given warmth and love. For three years the tree's fruits are *orlah* (forbidden to be eaten) and in the fourth year, the first fruits are to be given to Hashem.

"But what would happen to a plant if it were left to grow without guidance?

"It would grow slowly, and it would grow wild branches.

"So it is with a man.

"When he's a baby, he can't speak. But when he's three, he learns the letters, and then he learns to read, and at five, he studies Chumash.

"A child who grows without guidance may develop *chutzpadik*, unpleasant behavior, and then it will be very difficult for him to straighten himself out. Just as a plant needs to have its wild, crooked branches pruned, so does a child's behavior have to be closely supervised, and he must be carefully educated.

"Parents also have to learn how to educate their children, just as a gardener learns how to prune branches without harming the plant.

"After a tree is grown and gives fruit, we recite a blessing on the fruit to thank Hashem for all the good He gave us.

"Some trees don't give fruit. Even though they are barren trees, we still benefit a lot from them. They are beautiful to look at, and give us shade on a sweltering day."

"The fruits are the children of the tree?" the children asked.

"Yes! The fruits are the tree's children."

"And what if the fruits are rotten?" asked the little one.

"Then the tree is sad!" said my oldest son.

"Of course the tree is sad if the fruits are not good," I said, "just like a mother who raises her children and puts everything into them, and then sees they're not behaving. It's sad!"

Of all the plants we noticed on our way, I decided to spend the most time on the grapevine. Because of what our Sages say about an engrafted vine, I decided to explain to my children the connection between the grapevine and its offshoots.

One of the amazing qualities of a grapevine is that it creates new vines by sending its roots into the ground. *Chazal* explored the question: How can we determine the age of a grapevine with reference to the laws of *orlah*, since one cannot see when the grapevine sends forth its roots?

Chazal carefully studied the vine and reached an interesting conclusion. They found that as long as the offshoot is still receiving its nourishment from the original vine, and still needs it, the leaves face away from the parent vine (out of shame, *Chazal* tell us!). Only when the small vine matures and receives its nourishment from the ground independently do its leaves turn to face the original vine. *Chazal* learn from here an important lesson concerning gratitude. As long as a person is dependent on another for his living, he is ashamed to look him in the face.

Gratitude is a fundamental quality which must be inculcated in children. Every person in the world receives wonderful things from Hashem which give him strength to continue living. A person must learn how to show gratitude to his Creator. A person is given much power, and to the degree that he learns how to use it according to the Torah's way, so will he be useful to the entire universe. That's why a person's head faces upward — because his spiritual nourishment is from Heaven. We receive and give in the spirit of the Torah.

WHEN SUFFERINGS COME UPON a person, his sensitivity becomes sharpened — particularly if he doesn't try to rebel against his troubles but rather to figure them out. It's not easy at all. The bitterness is often overwhelming, and sometimes tips the scales. The bitterness overwhelms because life is hard.

"Who is making life so difficult for me?" I asked myself more than once. "Why is life so difficult?"

As I delved into this question, I broke it down into three:

1. Has Hashem's abundance lessened for me, or, God forbid, for the whole world?
2. Am I able to benefit from the abundance? Have I made myself a vessel to receive what Hashem wants to lavish on me? Or maybe I'm still kicking and don't want to accept any of the various "excuses" I have heard to explain my suffering.
3. What about the people around me? Can they absorb such a blow when it falls in their path?

Asking these questions helped me tremendously and opened my eyes. The main answers I found in Scriptures. I quickly realized that while HaKadosh Baruch Hu struck me with a terrible blow, at the same time He sharpened my senses, opened my heart, and drew me near to Him. I was very close to Him. I could ask Him for anything without being ashamed. More than once I waited for Him to answer me and He answered.

During those difficult days, I prayed that He shouldn't forsake me and that I shouldn't need anyone else. I wanted my living to come only from His open, warm, blessed, encompassing, and immeasurable Hand. And He answered me. Indescribably.

After my daughter's marriage, right before Pesach, Rav Manat phoned me and tried to ask me very tactfully and respectfully, "How are you managing? Do you need a loan?" The Rav realized that I had just made a wedding and now, right before the holiday, I surely could use some money.

So I told him, "Honorable Rav, when King David prayed to Hashem, he said, 'Like a suckling on its mother, so is my soul like a suckling.' When a baby nurses from his mother, he doesn't know how much to nurse; he doesn't know if his mother has enough for him. But he's completely trusting and secure; he doesn't even wonder whether there's enough milk for his needs.

"Do you know the peace of mind of a baby as he rests against his mother? There is no milk until he nurses. But as soon as he begins to nurse — the milk begins to flow. As much as you nurse, that much the blessing flows!

"Rav Manat, every time my children come to me and ask, 'Imma, give us money for a popsicle!' or 'Imma! I want to go on a trip!' I go into a corner and say to HaKadosh Baruch Hu, 'Ribono shel Olam, look! You see what I need money for. Should I hold this back from them?' And then HaKadosh Baruch Hu sends me another client to buy flowers, and I make just the profit I need!"

That's exactly how I felt. I never asked to become rich, only to make a decent living. However, I once was stunned by an encounter which left an impression on me that has remained to this day.

While I was sitting and making flower arrangements, a woman entered. She was on her way to buy a lottery ticket and her children had tagged along with her. They were also going to fill out a lottery ticket, and they, too, were going to wait tensely and excitedly for the day of the drawing. I was placidly sitting and arranging the flowers when she approached me and said, "Hello! How are you doing? I didn't know that you won the grand lottery prize!"

"I did? When?"

"After your husband passed away. Right after he died."

"Me? I never bought a lottery ticket in my life! Haven't I got anything else to do?"

"Are you trying to tell me that someone just made this up?" she said in puzzlement.

"*I* never heard that I won anything! Who made up such a bizarre story?"

The woman smiled and said, "Everyone knows it."

"This is weird. This is truly bizarre," I said. "Do I need to give my Creator advice on how to provide for me? Why the lottery of all things? Perhaps He wants to supply my livelihood in a different way!"

The woman left me astonished. I felt terrible confusion. For me, it was a real slap in the face. I had never been attracted to buy into this foolishness. Hungering for a lottery win allows a person no rest; it leaves him hanging in the air from one ticket to the next. I could never understand how people bring along their children when buying this futility, which in essence educates them to gamble. I don't know what the Halachah says about it and I never took the trouble to clarify the issue. I imagine that it's permitted, but how could it not corrupt the soul in some way when a person pins all his hope on a ticket? How can one even pray "Heal us" or "May our eyes behold Your return in mercy to Zion" sincerely, if all his yearnings are directed to winning the grand prize? I was truly confounded.

Afterwards, I felt humiliated. Why do people invent things about a person instead of just leaving him alone? They always have to spread stories around!

But then I felt pity. Pity for those people who don't know how much Hashem's Hand caresses us. They only see the Hand that smites, but not the Hand that heals. They meddle in another's wounds instead of sitting and digging into their own souls, searching out their flaws, and working out strategies to correct them.

I am dependent on You
By a thin thread
So thin
A thread of chesed
That turns nothingness into possibility
That lifts up from the dust.

I am dependent on You
By a puzzling thread
Of my only soul
Transparent
Flimsy

*But not worthless
At a special time of mercy*

*Hold me firmly to Your bosom
Until I return to You
My God!*

I ONCE READ THAT THE dead take part in the celebrations of their children.

I was particularly looking forward to my daughter giving birth. She told me that she was supposed to give birth the day before Pesach. If that's what would happen, and if it would be a son, the *brit* would be held on *Yom Tov*, on the seventh day of Pesach.

I shopped twice and even three times more than usual for Pesach. I purchased huge quantities of meat, fish, chicken and matzah, so if, God willing, it were a boy, we could celebrate the *seudat mitzvah* of a *brit milah* properly.

She gave birth on the day they had predicted. HaKadosh Baruch Hu bestowed on us a precious baby boy. The young couple gave me the honor of choosing both the *mohel* and the infant's name. I knew they were wonderful, but to such an extent! When I told them of my desire to call the baby Tzion Chaim, they were pleased and said they had also thought of that name.

But whom should I take for the *mohel*? I went back and forth on this issue. Of course, my thoughts wandered straight to my deceased Tzion. If he were alive, whom would he have chosen to circumcise his first grandchild? I finally decided on a Rav in our neighborhood who was known for his many acts of *chesed*. I informed the Rav of my decision, but still didn't feel at peace with it.

But then an amazing thing happened. The day before the seventh day of Pesach — the day before the *brit* — my son-in-law went to pray the *Shacharit* service in the synagogue where the Rav-*mohel* prayed. Right after *Shacharit*, the Rav approached him and said, "I had an important dream."

He told him that in his dream, Tzion *zt"l* had come to him and said, "I have a fine present to give you, but it's not ready yet." He then showed him circumcision tools and said, "Prepare the present with these tools."

My son-in-law came home and related the dream. I was excited. I hadn't told a soul about my ambivalence. But now HaKadosh Baruch Hu had anticipated my feelings and sent me verification from Heaven. The *mohel* himself had dreamed of the deceased grandfather.

Joy radiated through me and emptied me of all the fatigue and tension that had built up in me during the last few days. I knew that Tzion's pure spirit was present in our house, joining in our happiness. Suffused with tranquility and peace of mind, I cooked, baked, made the preparations, and set the table. I understood now more than ever the meaning of eternal life, and that the connection between souls is strong and indomitable.

Since Tzion's death, we had celebrated two happy affairs — the wedding of my daughter and the bar mitzvah of my dear son. On those occasions too, I had seen in a dream my deceased husband floating through the house. As guests arrived for Shabbat in my dream, I saw him place the water kettle on the Shabbat hotplate. "I'm here," he said. "Don't worry."

I thought then that my dream was merely an outgrowth of my thoughts, but now it was truly confirmed by the Rav's dream that these were not just false illusions.

IT WAS A WONDERFUL COMFORT to know that Tzion's spirit was truly with us. But nevertheless, a question sawed naggingly through the air: why hadn't our prayers for his recovery been accepted? We had prayed so hard. We had carried out so many vows, fasts, and resolutions for the future. We tried to arouse mercy in every way possible. So why weren't we answered?

I knew this question would be asked. How could it not be asked? I knew that the day would come when my children would also ask me that question: Imma, why?

Many scenes from my life passed in front of my eyes, scenes in which I had called out from a darkened corner, begging Hashem for His mercy. The prayers I had said when Tzion went to battle at the front, and when he did reserve duty in dangerous places. The prayers for livelihood, for health, for life. But one scene from all the scenes of my life always floated ahead and lit this dark corner, the corner where this question dominated.

I was then a young mother, only twenty years old. In my arms I held my daughter, who was just four months old. It was during the days preceding the Six Day War and the atmosphere was somber. It seemed as if one could cut the air with a knife, the atmosphere was so thick with tension and fear.

My daughter was suffering from a growth in her arm which was benign, but nevertheless dangerous. She had received radiation for two months, but the results were wretched. Her arm began to decay.

The young baby shrieked in pain. I was called back to the hospital urgently for consultation with the medical team. Terrified, I knocked on the door, my baby in my other arm.

"Mrs. Chubara," they said, "we have made every effort to help your daughter, but the radiation has injured her arm and damaged the blood vessels. As a result, the arm hasn't healed and there's a strong likelihood of general toxic poisoning. It is a question of life and death. We have no choice. To save your daughter's life, we must amputate her arm."

At first, I was stuck to my seat, speechless, trying to absorb what I had just heard. But then I stood up and said decisively, "No! I won't let you do this! Absolutely not!"

"Don't you understand that this is a question of life and death, and will determine what happens in the next twenty-four hours?"

"I don't understand anything. But it's clear to me that I can't accept your decision."

"If so, please sign here," one of the doctors told me.

I signed and left.

I threw myself onto a bench outside the room, totally stunned. I couldn't absorb all the things that were happening. I was completely alone at the time. My husband had been in the army for the past three weeks, like the rest of the country's male population. He didn't know anything, and I had no way of reaching him. My elderly parents lived far away. There was no point in worrying them. My mother-in-law wasn't feeling very well, in addition to being tense with worry. All three of her sons had been drafted into combat units; how could I add to her anxiety?

What should I do? Should I let them amputate my little daughter's arm?

Absolutely not!

But what about the poisoning? Life... death...

The corridor was dark and all the doors facing me were locked. No one moved through the corridor. The hospital was almost empty because they had readied it for war casualties, God forbid.

I held my daughter close to me. My tears fell non-stop. It was comforting for me to remain there, in that dark place, and release my emotions. I was alone with my baby and my Creator. I told Hashem, "You commanded us, 'Be fruitful and multiply.' You commanded it in the holy Torah. This is my first daughter. Is this Your blessing to me? Is this how one gives first fruits? Such a gift — Blemished? It is too difficult for me to accept this! I simply can't! That's all — I just can't!

"Please — give me just one hint what I should do. Whom should I go to for advice? The doctors have given their opinion, but they are

When Shivah Ends 115

only messengers. You created the arm! You and only You!"

My daughter was completely quiet the entire time, as if someone had whispered to her that right now a private session was going on with the *Shechinah*, and she mustn't interrupt.

"Ribono shel Olam! You know what, Ribono shel Olam? I'll try an experiment. I'll play with the fingers of that hand, and if... if the fingers begin to move, it's a sign that I'm right. But if, God forbid, the fingers stay rigid like a stone and don't react, I'll be forced to accept the Heavenly decree."

I sat in that dark corridor alone. I took my daughter's right palm, and began to play with the fingers. The sickly fingers didn't respond.

I continued, "Please, Hashem, You are the Healer of all flesh! You move the orb of the sun! You make all the winds blow! You bring down rain. What is it for You to bring the dead back to life?"

The fingers still didn't move.

"Ribono shel Olam! You asked us to bring a gift of first fruits from the very best, choicest crops! I was privileged to receive a gift of *bikkurim* from You, but is this the best?"

Another few minutes passed, several more tears, and then — the fingers... the fingers... two fingers began to move. Slowly.

It happened! A miracle!

The child laughed with her beautiful eyes, and I felt that from now on, everything would begin to change.

I met with a doctor, a professor who was considered an expert in the field of plastic surgery. I felt like one for whom a window had opened, and a fresh wind had filled my lungs. He received me warmly. I looked very young, and apparently, very distraught.

"How old are you, little girl?" he asked.

"I'm the mother. I'm twenty."

"Yes, but still a child! Why are you so distraught?"

He had touched my soul.

"Please, Professor! This is a question of life or death, involving my baby's right arm! I don't understand anything. Examine her yourself and tell me how you can help me."

I tried to be brave. I bit my lips and restrained my tears. He checked the arm and then said with a smile, "Don't worry. It's nothing. I'll try to cure her. It's just a matter of a serious infection."

He rubbed in thick layers of antibiotic ointment on the arm. A strong smell spread through the room. Every two days he would have to change the bandage, and in the meantime — we went home.

On the fourth night, when the doctor opened the bandage, he discovered that the infection had become worse. Again the arm was in danger.

"I need your husband immediately!" he told me.

"How can I bring him to you? He was drafted."

The doctor provided me with a letter. I approached the Schneller army base in Jerusalem, and within a day my husband arrived at the hospital. I knew they were hiding a big secret from me, but I wasn't inquisitive. I had no more strength left. I just prayed.

The next morning, they brought me to the operating room. My husband stood at my side. By then, he knew what they were going to do. And he told me, "The doctor is going to try to save the arm. He will try to make a skin transplant. But since the child is so young, they can't predict the operation's chance of success."

After the operation, my husband returned to the army and I remained with her in the hospital another twelve days. In the meantime, the Six Day War broke out. We prayed. And prayed. And prayed.

In my heart, I felt a special joy. A private joy. Concerning my daughter, I was sure that the wonderful revelation I'd had in the dark corridor would continue its blessing. But deep inside, fear encompassed all the Jews. We prayed for salvation.

On the twelfth day, my husband came home again for a few hours. He was again called to the operating room. There, I realized, he was told grave, worrisome things, words which I wanted to be insulated from. As far as I was concerned, they could talk all they wanted. I had my own special covenant, a covenant with the *Shechinah*, from back in that dark corridor.

Every doctor in the hospital was awaiting the results of that second operation. We later found out that this was the first operation of its kind in the world, in which this type of skin transplant had been done on a four-month-old baby.

Five hours later, our doctor burst out of the operating room, breaking into shouts of joy. He hugged my husband and then rushed through the entire hospital, telling his colleagues all about the operation. It was a wonder!

We went in to see the wonder: New skin had grown on my daughter's arm. Unbelievable! The arm was completely healthy. The fingers were still frail, but alive, *baruch Hashem*! She had an arm! A complete arm! It was Hashem showing His strong arm!

Eventually I found out that the operation had been publicized in the media. We were later invited back to the hospital, to have our picture and our baby's picture taken, for publication in an American medical journal.

The operation was very courageous and innovative, and Hashem's blessing rested upon our doctor.

One day several years later, I heard on the radio that he had suddenly died while on a trip abroad. That day I wept many tears for this man, remembering his beautiful personality and his strong desire to help others.

May his soul be bound up in eternal life.

This was an example of an open miracle. But what about all the big and small miracles that we experience every second? What about the miracles that we see, and those which we don't see? Do we always need a special miracle and special proof to know that our prayers have been accepted? Just the fact that we're here in the world — isn't that a wonder and miracle?

The soul in the fount of wisdom. It resides within the mind as a king amidst his battalions. It partakes partially of the glory of its Creator, so that it spurns the delights of men and the vanities of their amusements and generates wisdom and knowledge. All of its thoughts are to serve the Holy One Blessed be He in fear, and it contemplates what will transpire in the end, when the body dies and deteriorates, and how it will return in purity to Him Who created it and placed it within the body.
(Orchos Tzaddikim, Sha'ar Yiras Shamayim)

AFTER TZION'S PASSING, I WAS invited to Professor Nissan's office for a short consultation. Professor Nissan wanted to know how the disease had affected Tzion: had he been nervous, irritable? I was stunned by the question.

Professor Nissan then explained: "The liver is the chemical laboratory of the body, and its function is to filter out all the poisonous materials or to convert them to helpful substances. If the liver isn't functioning properly, the poisonous chemicals continue to flow in the blood and reach the head, where they cause headaches, make a person feel fuzzy, and simply drive him mad. A person going through this acts frenzied."

Then I understood.

Tzion had a sick liver for years. He had five years of terrible headaches and it was hellish. But when he suffered a rage attack such as Professor Nissan was talking about, he would go into his room and shut himself up for a long time. He wouldn't let those dreadful pains destroy the peaceful life that existed between us. He knew how to maintain his human dignity and knew at those terrible times how to make a separation.

For those rare times when he had become hysterical, he apologized profusely afterwards, and said, "I don't know what happened to me; I was in a fog."

Of course we complained to the doctors about those rage attacks, but at the time, the doctors' investigations had been in a completely different direction. His blood picture was borderline and didn't seem to indicate cancer.

Tzion's inner values helped him overcome chemical reactions that could have plunged him into insanity. His great soul and his wisdom ruled over his physical organs and overcame every illness, because his soul's entire goal was to return in purity to the One Who had created it and put it into that body.

Stories About Tzion zt"l

How did he have the strength to put up with such suffering? I asked myself many times. How did Tzion have the strength to bear so much physical pain while clearly knowing that in a short while he would leave us? Didn't he suffer the anguish of bidding farewell?

ALREADY FROM TZION'S FIRST operation — after they had removed the pancreas, gall bladder, and most of the liver from his body — he suffered hellish torments. Since his condition was so critical, they couldn't give him strong painkillers, and the dosage they did give him was too low. He was attached to dozens of machines that choked him, pressed on him, and stabbed him as they siphoned off the contaminated fluids.

Besides all this physical suffering, he was by nature a person of tremendous emotional intensity. He loved us very much. Just the terrible dread of having to bid his loved ones farewell would have been enough to drive anyone mad.

How did he bear it all? How did this man have such mighty strength?

These questions scrambled back and forth in my mind. I wanted to see everything clearly, to delve into every detail I knew, and to gather and combine it all together to reach a conclusion. From the answer I could derive clear-cut knowledge about the very purpose of a human being. I mustn't think lightly of the things I had seen. I must investigate them, examine them and learn from them, and God willing, also teach them.

And then, when combining the stories and the many details of Tzion's deeds going back to his youth, I understood that to become a hero like this requires lifelong toil. This is the toil one does in one's heart, one's true striving.

Our Sages tell us, "A person is known by three things: his cup, his pocket, and his anger" (*Eruvin* 65b). By his cup — when under the influence of alcohol, or (in our case) when his mind becomes addled by illness. When a man is not in control, words escape his mouth, and those words teach a world about him. The amazing thing about Tzion was that all the words he said during this period were very spiritual.

And so, in order to learn and to teach, I would like to relate here several stories from the many which I saved in my diary and in the cassette recordings that I made during the Shivah.

Judging Others Favorably

One of Tzion's most outstanding qualities was that he always judged people favorably.

Once, after we'd bought a building's roof rights, planning to build our apartment on the roof, one envious person decided to make our life miserable. He caused us tremendous distress, shouting at us, threatening us, and so on. One day I dreamt that that man was pursuing me with a gun. I was then in the last trimester of a pregnancy. When I got up I said to Tzion, "What does that wicked man want from us?"

As soon as he heard me say, "wicked man", Tzion raised his voice and said, "I've told you before that one doesn't evoke accusations even against wicked Jews… and certainly not against this man. There's an old lady who lives in his neighborhood, and who knows, maybe he treats her kindly. Maybe he once fixed her faucet. How can you call him a wicked man?"

Charity and Lovingkindness

David Tzarfati once told us, "When I was drafted, I was ordered to join a certain unit. It was a very united group. The members of the unit were on the ball and intelligent, and almost all of them were from the upper crust of society. I came from a moshav where all the residents were Moroccan immigrants, and our mentality was completely different. I spoke a pidgin Hebrew. I felt like an outsider in the unit.

"I'll never forget with what softness and sensitivity Tzion approached me and asked, 'Would you like to sit with me to study Hebrew? I also make a few mistakes, so we may as well study Hebrew together. You won't be insulted if I correct your mistakes, will you?'

"He taught me with unsurpassed devotion and diligence how to speak and pronounce the words correctly, until I felt more confident with the group. During our service, he was always there to give me the advice I needed. Even after each of us went our own way, he stayed in touch with me."

🙠 🙠 🙠

Another story from the army:

One youth whose parents had both passed away when he was young told me something very moving.

"When we finished our army service, and each soldier was about to go his own way, Tzion came up to me and walked with me a long while, talking about this and that, and finally, he held out an envelope. He told me, "Look, my friend. Each of us is going to his own destiny. Most of us have parents waiting for us at home (Tzion's father had passed away several months before), but you'll be alone when you return home. I want to give you this envelope."

Inside the envelope was all of Tzion's savings from his army service.

🙠 🙠 🙠

Another story from the many acts of charity that he did:

One day, a family moved to his neighborhood from abroad. The country they were from was considered prosperous. They dressed fashionably, and everyone who saw them thought they were well off.

But Tzion picked up that the situation wasn't as it seemed. He noticed that when the head of this family stood in prayer, he was sad and depressed.

He kept his eye on the man until one day he finally asked him, "How can I help you?"

The man then told him an astonishing thing. He said that although he had been wealthy in his previous country, he didn't have a cent for the coming holidays. All of his savings had been seized by the anti-Semitic regime, and there was no telling if he would ever get his money back.

Tzion went home and brought this man a sum of money that enabled him and his family to celebrate the holiday amid joy and plenty like every other Jew.

This story shows that one can perceive the truth if he possesses sensitivity and a good eye. Woe to one who looks at his friend from the critical perspective of envy and rivalry.

Another amazing story:

It was Tu bi'Shevat night, just a week after Tzion had been discharged from the hospital after a stay of several weeks. He was very weak. But after he heard that his former roommate had passed away, he decided to go and comfort the family. I went along.

After visiting them, we decided to buy a heater. We were standing in the entrance of the shop, when suddenly Tzion saw a man from afar. He ran to him (I don't know how he had the strength to run) and then returned to me and asked, "Do you have any money?"

"I just have enough for the heater," I said. (Our financial situation was terrible at the time.)

"Let me have the money, please." He took the wallet and ran again to the man, who was waiting at the end of the street.

When he returned to the store, he was very pale. He told me, "I've had this man on my mind for several months. I couldn't go visit him, so Hashem brought him to me. He needs help."

We bought the heater with a post-dated check.

I learned from him that one should run to give.

That night, to our good fortune, our youngest son was born.

Here is another story that shows how, to Tzion, money was a means, not an end:

We were thinking of buying a car. One evening we found a car that fit our needs and made plans to pay for it the next day. That same night we heard that one of our friends was in a state of financial collapse. Immediately, we tried to collect money for him, but were bombarded with difficulties. So we decided that if HaKadosh Baruch Hu had made things happen this way, it would be better to save the man from total collapse rather than buy a car. And that is what we did. We gave all the money to him. Five years later, we finally bought a car out of savings that HaKadosh Baruch Hu had provided.

After my husband's passing, the man came and offered to repay me. By then, *baruch Hashem*, the man was comfortably off, and the money was of great assistance to me.

Praying with a Minyan

Tzion was particular to pray with a minyan even when he was very weak.

One day, when his temperature was soaring above 102° F, I suggested that he go lie down. I sent the children away so it would be quiet. Then our niece arrived. I asked her to speak quietly because Tzion was sleeping.

She told me, "How could that be! I just saw him outside the synagogue, putting a minyan together!"

"You must be mistaken!" I exclaimed. I went into his room and saw his pajamas tossed on the bed. He had gone out of the room. How important it was for him to pray with a minyan.

Accepting Suffering with Love

One of the times I saw him writhing in pain, I asked him, "How do you have the strength to bear this?" He replied, "Every time I feel overcome with agony, I think of the Holocaust, and the *tzaddikim* of that time who sanctified the Name of Heaven. Then the pains are a little easier to bear."

Another story:

During Chanukah, when he was hospitalized in Hadassah hospital in critical condition, he was writhing in agony after receiving an injection in his esophagus. I didn't know how to console him.

So I said, "Tzion, suffering atones for sins."

He replied, "Do you know when suffering atones for sins? Only when a person has in mind that his suffering should atone for his sins and he completely regrets them."

That's how sharp his thinking was. No action of his was devoid of thought; whatever he did was imbued with total intent.

Hospitality

Tzion loved people, and his love was especially evident on Shabbat and the holidays. Every Shabbat he made sure we had at least one guest. So our guests wouldn't feel they were a bother, God forbid, we set aside a room in our new house especially for guests. I'll never forget those Shabbatim when new faces appeared in our home. Once, when we had no guests, our children were upset and they asked us, "Why are you punishing us by not inviting guests?"

In the last month of his life, Tzion was very ill. He was worn out and sallow. One Thursday, the telephone rang and we were informed that two new *ba'alei teshuvah* would be coming. I hoped to Hashem that Tzion would feel better at least for Shabbat. But an hour before Shabbat his condition worsened, and his fever rose to almost 104 degrees.

I was heartsick. On one hand, I wanted our guests to feel welcome. I wanted them to taste what Shabbat was like in a religious Jewish home in the best way possible. But on the other hand, I realized that my husband was very sick. Who knew if he would be able to sit at the table at all?

That entire day, I felt anxious while preparing for Shabbat. Tears trickled from my eyes as I worked, begging Hashem all the while that at least in honor of Shabbat, Tzion should feel better.

I lit the Shabbat candles with trembling hands. Tzion was too weak to go to the synagogue and he was forced to pray at home. I made sure the children kept quiet.

And suddenly, when our guests returned from the synagogue after Ma'ariv, there was Tzion, coming out of his room dressed in his Shabbat clothes, with the familiar, lovely smile on his face. He said, "My fever is down. I'm joining you."

He made Kiddush and sat with us that entire Shabbat evening with a holy glow on his face, and with that gentleness which always radiated from him, especially on Shabbat. He ate a little mashed food (he had been unable to eat normal food for half a year already, because several times it had caused a tear in the veins of his esophagus).

I realized then, more than ever, that HaKadosh Baruch Hu also joins us at the table. So great is the mitzvah of hospitality, so great is it to help people return to their Creator, that Tzion's strength returned to allow him to do these wonderful mitzvot one more time. How could we have been a good influence on our guests, who were so thirsty for truth, without Tzion and his wonderful *divrei Torah*? That Shabbat I experienced, in a most concrete way, a miracle and a wonder.

Keeping One's Word

The following rather "run-of-the-mill" story shows how precious is a father's word.

It was 7:30 in the evening, and my husband had just returned from his learning. Running to him, our little son asked, "Abba, did you buy me a treat? You promised!"

But Abba said, "I'm sorry, I forgot."

"It's not the end of the world," I told my son. "Tomorrow, God willing, we'll buy you a treat."

Some time later, I noticed that Tzion had left the house. He returned twenty minutes after that, a candy bar in his hand.

"The child already forgot about it!" I told him. "You could have waited until tomorrow."

"No! I wanted to teach him the importance of a promise — the power of a spoken word."

※ ※ ※

When one of the children was sick, Tzion didn't let him sleep alone. He always took a mattress and slept on the floor next to the sick child for the night. We usually took turns.

He utilized every occasion to explain *halachot* to the children. "This is how Hashem wants us to do it," he would say. For instance, when he cut the children's nails, he explained the laws of nail-cutting, and similarly for tying shoes. He taught the children that every action is significant.

         🙠   🙠   🙠

The following stories testify to Tzion's integrity, sincerity, and gratitude.

When we built our house, we hired an Arab contractor from Abu Ghosh. He quoted a price which included all the expenditures for the construction and his wage. But, instead of charging us as all contractors did, he asked for the amount in a bizarre way. He told Tzion, "Look, I trust you. I have no time for bookkeeping. So I want you to manage the expenses, and pay the workers their wages every day. Likewise, you pay for the materials. When the project is finished, pay me the balance."

I was astonished. How could the contractor make such an offer? He didn't know anything about Tzion. How could he leave such a matter in his hands?

I felt that Tzion had made a great *kiddush Hashem*. He made an exact accounting, and to this day I have the notebook where he wrote all the accounts down. This shows how meticulous he was about interpersonal mitzvot, even when it involved non-Jews.

Honoring Parents

Gratitude was one of the qualities which were deeply embedded in him. It made him exude warmth and affection to all those around him.

Tzion used to visit his mother every day. He always checked to make sure everything was fine with her, and to see if she needed anything fixed in the house.

One day he didn't feel well so he didn't go to visit her. Instead, he phoned her up at 9:00 P.M. She sounded weak, but she said it was probably because she was tired. "I'll go to sleep and I'll feel better when I get up tomorrow," she said.

Tzion hung up the phone. After a few minutes, he got up, got dressed and said, "I don't feel right about Imma. I have to check what's going on with her."

When he got to her house, he took her temperature. It had climbed to 102° Fahrenheit.

He called Dr. Meshullam, who came right away. After examining her, the doctor sent her straight to the hospital for an urgent operation. Later, the doctor told us that if she had waited a little longer, it would have been too late to save her. Her life was saved by Tzion's sensitive intuition. That's when I saw what a real connection to a mother was.

Simplicity

Tzion was asked more than once, Why don't you wear a suit? You're a *ben Torah*. He would always reply with an evasive, humorous answer.

But to me he told the truth. He said, "If I wear a suit, people will think I'm a true *ben Torah*, who pores over his Torah study day and night. But since I don't devote my entire day to Torah, I don't want to put on a false front. People might give me honor that I don't deserve. I'm just a simple person, and therefore I have to dress simply.

He was also asked, "How come you don't have a title or a degree? You've studied Torah and science for many years!" He would again dismiss the question with humor. But he told me, "If I wanted to be a *dayan* in a Rabbinical court, I would need certification that I studied *dayanut*. If I wanted to be an engineer or a technician, I would need certification to prove my training. But since I'm studying *lishmah*, for the sake of the study alone, I don't need any certificates. Certificates would only make me more arrogant."

That was his chosen way. He studied in order to advance in the service and fear of God, not to get degrees and festoon himself with certificates. That's the kind of man he was.

Contemplation

One of Tzion's most wondrous traits was his ability to contemplate things around him.

Contemplation brings a person back to the moment of Creation, where he can see the awakening, the light, and the beauty. It shakes off the dust of routine living and removes the worry about tomorrow, for tomorrow belongs to the Creator of the Universe.

That's how Tzion maintained his vitality. He knew how to rejuvenate himself. His time was never empty, for every second was filled with pleasure. He knew how to stop, take a moment to gaze at a plant, and be captivated by its beauty. He reflected on ancient trees and on wildflowers. His personal taste was complex and delicate; he loved antiques as well as a contemporary look, both in art and architecture. He studied the beauty in man. He put his own hand to artwork, too; as a youth, he had embroidered a beautiful *parochet* for the Ramban synagogue.

His approach to life was unique, and because of that, he had an aversion to all flattery and unctuous expressions of respect. These were foreign to him, and he kept as distant from them as the South Pole is from the North.

On the last Friday we spent together at home (he was hospitalized for the final time that *motza'ei Shabbat*), he had just come back from the hospital when he met a neighbor walking about in his extensive garden. Tzion joined the neighbor, apologizing for not keeping his promise to help him plan the garden, and mentioned the names of flowers and plants that would thrive in this sunny spot, in that shady spot.

What a magnificent man! He was so sick then, so near to death... but he could still speak about planting, the beauty of nature, the sounds of the dawn. He always tried to imbibe from the Source, from nature, from the beauty of Creation. That's why he was always attracted to the good even when he was a little, innocent, and pure child. His face shone with truth.

Only such a person, who feels so closely connected to his Creator, understands that whatever is given to him in This World is a gift. Every second of life is a miracle. Only such a man, who constantly asks himself, "What does HaKadosh Baruch Hu ask of me today?", for whom this is the key question that guides his life... only such a person could lift himself up and push aside trappings of honor, flattery, the race after money and glitter. All the things that belong to a dark world, a world of falsehood.

Only such a person could return his soul like a one-day-old baby, to reunite with the Divine in awesome sublimity, dressed in his Shabbat clothes.

What a magnificent man.

IN THESE FEW HANDWRITTEN NOTES included here, you can see Tzion's struggle with the pen. I'll never forget how his hand shook when he wrote, and how much effort he exerted to express himself.

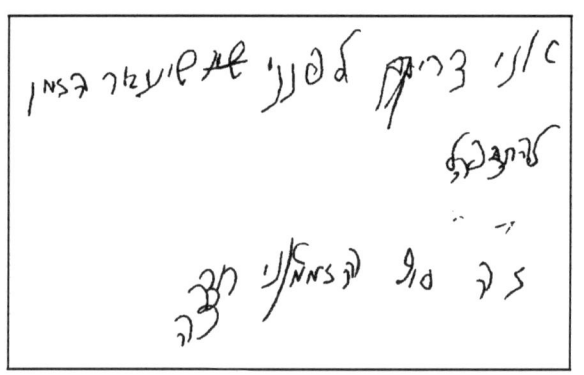

Tzion's struggle to make sure he put on his tefillin in the prescribed time. A doctor had arrived to treat Tzion, but Tzion asked him first to help him put on his tefillin:
"I need to pray before the time limit passes. It's the end of the zeman."

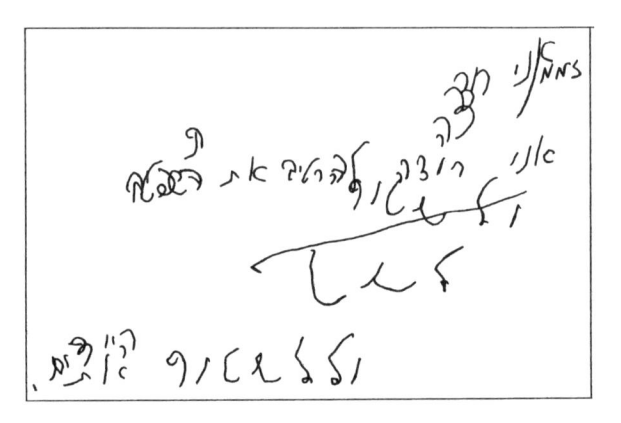

Tzion's trembling handwriting:
"I want to wet my lips and wash my hands."

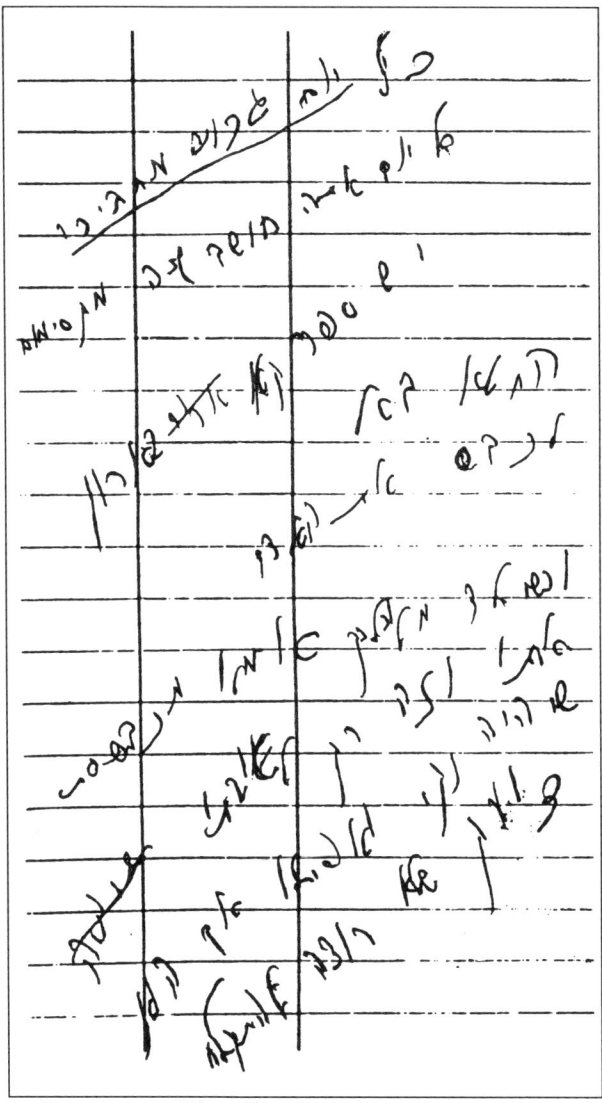

Tzion's trembling handwriting (the paper was stained with blood):
"Each day is worse than the one before. Each day you think, this is the worst it can get. There's a little book in the closet. Sin comes to cleanse a person. When a child is dirty, the mother washes him. It's only for his own good, so he'll be clean. Even if he screams that he doesn't want to take a shower."

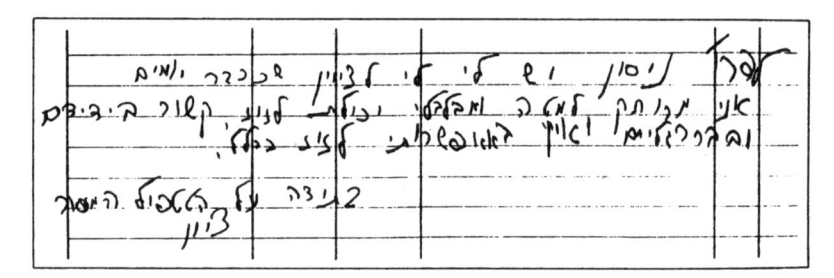

Despite his weakness and confusion, Tzion didn't forget to express himself politely to the doctor and thank him:
"Prof. Nissan, I have to mention that for two days already I can't move from the bed, my hands and legs are tied down, and I am unable to move at all. Thank you for your devoted care. Tzion."

"Bless me together with all other sick Jews."

Gratitude — a trait that gives strength during difficult moments:
"Baruch Hashem, Who has not ceased dealing kindly with me nor put an end to His kindnesses. Every day, you see His wonders. I also heard the voices of all the people outside praying, both young and old. I cannot stop thanking all those who are doing and enabling others to do this great thing. May they be blessed with everything good."

When a friend came to visit, Tzion asked in writing that a chair be brought for him. He gently explained to him what was happening, as if in apology:

"As you said, baruch Hashem, but how? No one knows. Only around 5:00 in the afternoon, it became clear to Prof. Nissan that the pressure had been lowered drastically. Until then everyone was unsure. Only half an hour ago another attempt was made. The respiratory and pressure machine broke between my teeth and stabbed my stomach like needles. I have another problem — my veins themselves are prickly because of a treatment I did 10 months ago in Kfar Saba.

"Prof. Nissan said that he never saw anyone like the religious and the newly religious studying in yeshiva when it comes to giving blood, especially right before Shabbat."

Tzion wrote this note in a hazy state. He repeats words, but is making an effort to honor his guest:

"Regards to everyone in the yeshiva, and thanks to each one. How I wish that I — or someone else — could give an abundance of good things in return to each of you."

A quote from the letter:
"I only want to cooperate. You assume that I don't understand a thing. From the beginning, I managed to cough by myself. Mostly, I get frantic when my needs are not being fulfilled. For instance, I am tied too tightly when it could be looser. I have to wash my hands, to put on tefillin. I'm always willing to accept what you say, from A to Z. It would be a shame to ruin our relations toward the end... another two weeks. One of my worst problems is my inability to speak. Sometimes I ask for a certain thing, and instead, I am given Valium."

How Does One Overcome?

In the following section, I have tried to indicate ways to help someone get over a tragedy. I tried to briefly answer questions that came up in conversations with people who had lost their loved ones. The subjects of vindicating God's judgment, a righteous man who suffers, etc., are broad and profound topics, and to do them justice, one would have to write many volumes. Therefore I only touched marginally on these subjects, for I am not qualified to deal with them in depth.

WHEN A PERSON IS in crisis, there are two paths he can take.

One path is easy but dangerous. To hold onto the grief, to guard it inside, to dig a deep hole and start moving steadily downward! It's impossible to know ahead of time where this path will lead you. A person sometimes sobers up in the middle, discovers that he has changed for the worse, and immediately wants to get out. If he is steering well and driving carefully, he won't be frightened by the stones on the road. There is a chance that he'll return to the point he started out from, and will even advance further. But if he doesn't wake up, whether because it's easier to stay where he is, because he's afraid, or because he is full of despair, he will continue plummeting, God forbid.

The second way is to take the pain in hand and try to make something sweet out of the bitterness. This way is much harder. It's like a person trying to reach the peak of a tall mountain. The mountain is steep and threatening. No one knows the best path to reach the summit, and no one knows what equipment is needed. You're afraid to start the climb up. What will happen if you stumble? From where will you get the strength to start again? These questions torment you and cause you distress day and night, and woe to one who allows himself to harp on them.

The only way to escape these questions and doubts is to get up and be active. That's all it takes. Just move your arms and legs and get going. And when you're active, don't expect a single thing. That way, every accomplishment you make will be recorded in your memory as a gain. Don't be afraid of falling, getting up again and going on, even if you stumble on the way.

One day, when the pain was again gnawing at me, and on the verge of making me fall, I discovered an amazing thing.

It happened one run-of-the-mill morning. After all my children had gone off, this one to kindergarten and that one to school, I went to my flower cabinet. (An expert carpenter had built it to store dried flowers. It was airtight; no moisture or air could seep in.) I took out several flowers and dry leaves. Among the leaves were some ferns. Their leaves were clear as glass, due to their having been treated with a special chemical solution and bleached with special whitening material. Their appearance was truly lovely. Since they were on the expensive side, I usually only used them to make a garland for a bride.

I got to work. As I looked closely at the leaves, I noticed tiny dark dots patterned in precise order along the length of each leaf's artery. I didn't know where these dots came from. I suspected that the leaves were developing a plant infestation, but I didn't spot any other signs which would indicate it. I put these sprigs in a plastic bag and stored the bag away from the cabinet so that the rest of my stock would not be infected. I decided to observe the leaves and see what would happen.

After a week, I noticed that a similar set of tiny black dots began to appear on the green ferns I was keeping in a vase — in the exact order in which they appeared on the white ferns. I then realized that these were seeds.

I was stunned — stunned at the vitality a plant possesses. This sprig of ferns had gone through a drying process, been soaked in a salt solution and bleached, spent time in dark surroundings, and been transported from abroad. It had also spent a year just lying in my cabinet before I finally decided to take it out and use it. And at exactly the same time that its water-saturated, sunlight-splashed, warm and pampered cousin was giving out seeds, at that very time the chemically treated fern, too, decided to cry out, "I'm still alive!"

It was a wonder to me. This is the power of Creation!

And I looked at myself and said, "Learn from this little leaf that quivers in your hand."

> *Better one action than a thousand groans.*
> *(R' Sholom Dov of Lubavitch)*

ANOTHER VERY IMPORTANT WAY to get over the pain is to do something in memory of the departed loved one. Since the dead cannot fulfill mitzvot in the world of souls, we can help raise them to a higher level through our good deeds. A son can give merit to his father by fulfilling mitzvot; he is commanded to follow in his father's good ways. Similarly, one can take upon oneself a resolution and keep it faithfully. Good resolutions benefit the departed, his family, and Jews everywhere.

Once the spark of activity is ignited in a person, he must utilize it without delay. He shouldn't worry that he may not succeed. He must believe that HaKadosh Baruch Hu will assist him.

I'll give an example. My children and I accepted upon ourselves a resolution to do something for the elevation of their father's soul. Hashem helped us in the best possible way, and our reward was very great. We felt a sense of continuity, joy, and spiritual exaltation.

The moment I returned home from the funeral, I had decided in my heart to do something to elevate the soul of our beloved one. I immediately asked my daughter to write an announcement concerning the opening of a crib *gemach* (a supply of cribs to be lent out free of charge to any family needing one) in Tzion's memory. We put this announcement at the entrance to our home, and our many visitors were asked to donate whatever they could. And people gave.

At the end of the Shivah, Rav Manat said to me, "Brachah, I think that in Tzion's memory, it would be more suitable to open a tefillin *gemach* for the newly observant who have not yet managed to purchase a pair [since good tefillin are quite costly], because Tzion *z"l* wrote tefillin parchments and was close to *ba'alei teshuvah* as well."

I told him that Tzion *z"l* had dreamt of a crib *gemach* while yet alive, but hadn't had a chance to bring the dream to fruition. However, Rav Manat thought it would be difficult for us to manage a crib *gemach* because it involved much lugging and storage space.

I thanked him for the idea. In the end, with the generous help of my brother-in-law, I set up a tefillin *gemach*. The money which the visitors had contributed was enough to purchase two fine, *mehudar* sets of tefillin, and my brother-in-law managed to prepare another eleven sets. To this day, he runs the *gemach* and makes sure the tefillin are repaired and the straps are replaced when necessary.

But the idea of a crib *gemach* wouldn't go away. For two months, I kept tossing and turning on my bed, very disturbed about the matter for two reasons: first, because the deceased had wished for it, and secondly, because I had promised the visitors who donated the money to set up a crib *gemach*, and perhaps they were expecting that cribs, and nothing else, would be bought with their money. I had no peace.

One day the phone rang in my house. It was Professor Bodenheimer, calling to tell me about the Apter and Shmayovitz families who had lost their babies, and in their memory, had set up a crib *gemach* in Shilo two years ago. Because of the distance from Jerusalem, where most of their "customers" lived, they were finding it difficult to maintain the *gemach*, and they were looking for a Jerusalemite who would agree to manage the *gemach*. Would I agree?

What a question! I jumped up from my seat. Heaven must have directed you to me, I thought.

The Apters and Shmayovitzes immediately brought me their cribs. We printed explanatory material and advertised, distributing our notices mainly in hospital maternity wards and in Mother and Baby clinics, and the *gemach* quickly doubled in size. We soon had about 200 items, including beds, carriages, cribs, and playpens.

My younger children became little activists, displaying knowledge and interest in everything that had to do with the *gemach*. Every now and then I would tell them about the birth of twins, triplets, or quadruplets. The excitement in our house whenever we heard such news was indescribable. People came to us full of joy, and gave us the feeling that we were true partners in their happiness.

Once again the children became aware that HaKadosh Baruch Hu desires a functioning world, and wants it to blossom. My oldest daughter did even more than the others. Several times, I saw her cleaning out the cribs. "How can we give a dirty crib to a new mother?" she would say. My nine-year-old son would phone people and remind them that it would soon be time to return the crib. Of course, if the family asked to use it longer, we gave permission.

More than once, cribs were not returned for several years. This was for the simple reason that the crib was needed by the family because *baruch Hashem* they had a child every year.

WHEN SOMEONE PRECIOUS IS taken from us, it's only natural to be flooded with memories and pictures from the past. We don't relive our memories only to remember what it was like when they were with us. Sometimes, we search our memories to learn from our dear departed one, to try and understand the messages he sought to impart.

For me, recalling those pictures was a painful, but constructive experience. I would try to take a memory and analyze it from all directions, while trying to neutralize my feelings. I forced myself to concentrate on the experience only, so that my observation would be clearer. Usually, this exercise helped me.

I'll give an example:

Tzion had his first operation on a Shabbat morning. He woke from it only on Monday afternoon, the eve of Tishah b'Av. I was still dressed in my Shabbat clothes, and seeing that it was late afternoon, he thought Shabbat was about to enter. His face shone with joy as he wrote, "*A little wine for Kiddush...lechem mishneh...sing something....*"

When I explained to him that it wasn't Shabbat, and the Tishah b'Av fast was almost here, he bit his lips, his face darkened, and tears flowed from his eyes. He wrote, "*Eicha yashvah badad*" (the opening words of the book of *Eichah*).

I thought a lot about this event. I learned from it the sanctity of time.

What difference does it make to a mortally ill person, who has been unconscious for three days, whose internal organs are in ruins — what difference does it make to him what day it is? Is he planning to go to synagogue with his children? Is he planning to sit down to a festive meal? Is he planning to break out in a dance?

What difference could it make? No food can pass his lips, he can't have wine to make Kiddush. In any event, he has been fasting one long fast, so what does it matter to him whether today is

How Does One Overcome?

Shabbat or Tisha B'Av? It was astonishing to me.

Then I remembered another event that had happened on the previous Fast of Gedalyah, almost a year before. Tzion had been hospitalized for three consecutive weeks, and was discharged before Rosh HaShanah for a short break. Rosh HaShanah falls on the first two days of Tishrei, and the Fast of Gedalyah is on the following day, the third of Tishrei. That year Rosh HaShanah occurred on Thursday and Friday, and since the next day was Shabbat, the Fast of Gedalyah was deferred until Sunday.

As is known, a sick person is exempt from fasting, all the more so for a fast that is deferred, and certainly for the Fast of Gedalyah, which is considered a minor fast (unlike Yom Kippur and Tisha B'Av).

On Sunday, after he returned from the morning prayers, I prepared a hot drink and a sandwich for him. We were supposed to go back to the hospital immediately, but Tzion refused to taste anything and said he had decided to fast.

We drove to the hospital. A doctor measured his blood pressure, and immediately attached him to the intravenous. Tzion, of course, continued to fast, claiming that it was even easier for him now since he was getting fluids anyway.

Looking back at this memory, I thought to myself, did he do right or not? If the Sages exempt someone like him from the fast, they must have a good reason for it! Now, as I thought of both events, I reached the conclusion that Tzion was living on a completely different level than I was.

Tzion sanctified time.

One who knows how to sanctify time also knows how to sanctify himself. He has only one goal: "You shall be holy, for I am holy…" (*Vayikra* 19:2). He didn't want to mortify himself, absolutely not! He was far from self-mortification. He simply lived for mitzvot, and the mitzvot kept him alive. And the proof of it was when he was in the Intensive Care Unit after that first operation. That's when I understood why it was so important to him to know which day it was: because even if he could do absolutely nothing external in observance of the day, he cared about its *essence*.

This shed light on another point for me:

Our Sages say that when a man is ill, the *Shechinah* hovers near his head. I felt how Tzion sensed the *Shechinah* in the Intensive Care Unit. Where the *Shechinah* is, it's impossible to speak idle words.

I felt this as well from the letter he wrote to Rav Alshich, *shlita*, when the Rav came to visit him. "*Baruch Hashem, Who has not ceased dealing kindly with me nor put an end to His kindnesses....*" The entire letter was a song of praise and thankfulness to God, Who had heard the community's prayers. This proved to me that a sick person knows and senses when others pray for him; and we, therefore, are obligated to contemplate this, and to pray with great devotion for the sick of Israel.

❧ ❧ ❧

Here's another thing that helped me very much:

From the moment that I decided to accept the Heavenly judgment, from the second that I understood that I'm nothing when it comes to understanding what happened and why it happened, I was infused with strength.

Rav Mordechai of Lechowitz said a wonderful thing: "Without HaKadosh Baruch Hu, one can't cross the threshold of one's house. But with HaKadosh Baruch Hu, one can split the sea."

It's so true that without Hashem, we can't even cross the threshold of our house... so how can we complain to the Master of the Universe? Instead of filling our heads with unnecessary, perplexing thoughts, we should be purifying our heart with faith, and let that faith rejuvenate us. Bitter things can be made sweet by sprinkling salt on them.

HaKadosh Baruch Hu's greatness cannot be perceived through probing, but only through faith. We must remember that one of the most important questions a person is asked when he reaches the Upper World is: "Did you occupy yourself with faith?" What will we answer the Ribono shel Olam then?

Another way:

To learn Torah… to learn and learn some more! To constantly learn Torah.

ALL MY PONDERINGS ABOUT THE meaning of life, and what man's role in the world is, intensified after we lost our precious Tzion. We tried together, my children and I, to deal with these questions.

We are all created by God, I told my children, formed of a spirit and a body. My children often asked me, "Imma, why is there such a big difference between people? Everyone is built from the same material!"

It was a lovely, simple question, yet I had to consult our holy books before I felt ready to answer it.

I explained to them that human beings have many contradictory qualities. People have lofty traits, such as truthfulness, mercy, and kindness. However, they also have negative qualities, such as dishonesty, cruelty, and stinginess.

Hashem made us different from all other creatures by giving us free will, and through this we are taught that we are even greater than angels. A person can choose his path. Free will gives us a sense of power, knowing that it is up to us whether we'll be gentle, pleasant people, or the opposite.

This power gives rise to a great contradiction. People can think that they have only themselves to thank for whatever they have achieved: "My strength and the power of my hand brought me this success." Yet how ridiculous this is when we merely consider how a microscopic virus can make a person as weak as a fly. From where is man's strength then?

Our strength comes from our Divine gift of intelligence. Through it, we can rise above our animal desires and reach sublime heights of understanding and knowledge — knowledge of Torah, and knowledge of the world we live in.

I told my children that we can see the wonders of Creation in the harmony that exists in every cell of a plant or an animal. The wisdom embedded in a living creature, which we call "instinct," is a tremendous wonder. It is astonishing to see the migrations of birds and fish to far-off places which particularly suit them because of the temperature and abundant food supply in these locations. It's amazing to see their hidden senses in action, their ability to sense imminent danger and to flee from it.

It is incredible that a plant strikes roots in the direction where it "knows" it will find water and the elements it requires for its nourishment. And what about a plant's attraction to light? Even if it is placed in a dark room, its leaves will stretch out in the direction from which a tiny point of light will most likely appear.

This is all the more true of human beings. A person's brain is a wonder, with an incredible capacity for thought and perception, and although everyone's brain has the same physical structure, each brain has its own unique attributes which determine the person's individual personality. This is a God-given gift to mankind, an amazing, marvelous gift. Therefore, I told my children, it is important for them to develop their capacity for thought and understanding, and to direct it to the service of Hashem.

Avraham Avinu, the father of the Jewish people and the son of Terach the idol-worshiper, discovered his Creator on his own. From Avraham we learn that if a person applies his power of thought and deduction correctly, he can arrive at faith through his own efforts.

I reminded my children that we were also created with a heart, to guide us in using our human attributes wisely and humbly, rather than arrogantly. We must listen to our heart, and do good deeds that will bring *nachat* to our Creator and His creations. Connecting with our Creator is our desire and our duty.

When a person suffers from a physical ailment, I explained, he does his utmost to find the best doctor and take the necessary medications, cost notwithstanding. He'll do anything he has to do, to recover. We should feel the same concerning our bad personality traits, our "spiritual ailments." We should learn how to recognize them and do our best to "recover" by uprooting them. This is not easy; our Sages tell us that it is easier to learn the entire Talmud than to uproot one bad personality trait!

A person is not born because he wants to be born. Whether he likes it or not, he is alive! Whether he likes it or not, he will die!

Whether he likes it or not, in the future he will have to give a reckoning in the World of Truth. In this, there is no free will. Sorrow and tragedy may afflict his life. The question is, how to understand it, how to experience it, how to draw closer to Hashem through it.

> *I would definitely not want to serve*
> *a God Whose ways are comprehensible*
> *to the minds of human beings.*
> *(R' Menachem Mendel of Kotzk)*

WHAT IS DEATH? I PONDERED. A kind of birth?

There are three kinds of "birth": conception in a mother's womb; emergence from a mother's womb into the world; and departure from the world.

We have an eternal tie to the earth, because we are made of earth. Why, then, are we so bewildered and frightened by death? What are we afraid of?

We fear the unknown. The secrecy of death weighs down on us. The rendezvous with death means that one day our ego will be annulled. The thought of our ego vanishing terrifies us, until we learn the meaning of death.

"Those who are born will die, and those who are dead will live" (*Pirkei Avot* 4:22). This means that one who dies goes on to eternal life.

We act very strangely: When a baby is born, we rejoice. We're very happy. But do we know at that moment what kind of life the baby will have? Will he be content or, God forbid, will he have a life of suffering? Will he be righteous or wicked? Will he bring blessing to the world or, God forbid, a curse? None of this is known when a child is born.

On the other hand, when a person dies, we weep, and feel anguish and pain. But do we know where he went? Perhaps he entered a completely blessed world and we should rejoice for him that he attained the eternal life of Gan Eden.

The Hebrew letters *ayin-lamed-mem* (עלם) denote both "world" and "hidden." As much as we have discovered the order and harmony in the world, the secrets of this world remain concealed. The more we observe Creation, the more we see that This World was intended to be a blessing and not, God forbid, a curse, that it was made for fulfillment, not destruction, and the more evident it becomes that our Creator's intention was for good.

In This World, the soul is within the body. The soul longs to attain knowledge of Hashem, to cleave to Hashem, while the body confines and hinders its perceptions. The more the soul exerts itself, the more it acquires the perception of Hashem, and the higher is its spiritual level. Even after it leaves the body, we are taught, it is uplifted to a more sublime existence in the World to Come, commensurate with the perception it attained in This World. At that point, it will be able to perceive far more exalted matters.

The *Talmud Yerushalmi* says, "During the first three days [after death], the soul hovers over the body...." This means that the soul longs to return to the body. For the entire seven days of Shivah, the week of mourning, the soul flits between the grave and the home, for it finds parting painful.

Rav Yosef Yehudah Leib Bloch *zt"l* asks in his book, *Shiurei Da'at*: What does it mean that "the soul hovers over the body"? Does it not know, as every man knows, that death is a final parting? He explains that the concepts of "time" and "place" belong to our physical world and are non-existent in the Upper World, where everything is perceived spiritually. Even though we use the terms "Lower World" and "Upper World," it is actually all one world, but perceived at different levels.

We can illustrate the difference with an example from our world, the corporeal world. Imagine a tiny ant. What does it know of our world and our affairs? Because its powers are so limited, an ant cannot comprehend us and our world. This is true on a physical level, and it is even truer concerning emotions.

These two entities — a human being and an ant — live in the same world! Nevertheless, we do not experience it as the same world. Likewise, when the soul leaves the body, it perceives This World differently. It recognizes, sees, understands all the phenomena of the world completely differently. Its perception is still limited and far from ultimate reality, yet this perception is sublime compared to our earthly level.

The Talmud tells us (*Berachos* 8a): "Nine hundred and three kinds of death were created in the world." What does this mean? Our Sages say that a person's experience of death depends on what his connection to This World is like. The more he is connected to material things, the more difficult he finds death. Those who followed paths of righteousness in This World will see their souls continuously elevated from one world to the next. They will delight in infinite Divine light and bliss.

May our portion be with them!

Vindicating Judgment

WE ARE TAUGHT THAT BEFORE we leave this world, we should contemplate our deeds, repent, and vindicate every judgment of Hashem.

When we are in distress, our soul can become very bitter. We might, God forbid, question Hashem's decisions, and rebel against our suffering. Therefore, when all is going well for us, we should accustom ourselves to appreciate all that God gives us. If deep gratitude is ingrained in our soul, we will also be able to accept with love whatever tribulations may come our way.

We can learn from Iyov's astonishing acceptance of suffering (*Iyov* 2:9–10):

> His wife said to him, "How can you still maintain your wholehearted devotion? Why don't you blaspheme *Elokim* and die?" But he replied, "You are speaking like a wanton woman! Shall we take the good from *Elokim* but not the bad?" In all this Iyov did not sin with his lips.

Gittin 28a recounts a moving story about a young child who was taken captive by the Romans:

> Rabbi Yehoshua ben Chananya went to a large city in the Roman empire. There he was told about a lovely child with beautiful eyes and curly hair who was in prison.... Rabbi Yehoshua asked the child, "Who allowed Yaakov to be trampled and Israel to be plundered?" The child replied, "Was it not Hashem against Whom we sinned?" Rabbi Yehoshua said, "I am sure that he will become a judge in Israel! I will not move from here until I redeem him for any sum which they demand."

Here a little child vindicated his own suffering! Without any hope of redemption, his belief remained unfaltering, no doubt because of the outstanding education he had received in his parents' home. It gave him the strength to withstand great suffering, and led to his redemption.

Weeping

WHY DO WE WEEP AFTER the death of a dear one?

We read in *Yirmeyahu* (22:10):

> Do not cry for the dead and do not be agitated over him. But you should surely cry for the one who is going, for he will never return.

Who are those who are "*going*"? They are those who are still alive in This World and are progressing toward their own death. Will they die righteous or, God forbid, wicked? Concerning those who are already dead, if they died righteous, why should you cry over them?

And yet, we do cry. Why?

We cry because of the *void* left behind when a righteous person passes away. We cry because of *our loss*.

The question is asked, can we weep if the weeping comes from self-pity? An even more basic question: Why do we want to cry? Why were tears created? What is the meaning of our Sages' statement, "The gate of tears is never locked" (*Berachot* 32b)?

The Maharal explains, "Tears are a testimony to the puniness and powerlessness of man, which he is never prevented from expressing." This means that if we humble ourselves before Hashem and demonstrate our complete self-effacement, powerlessness, and submission to His will, placing His will before our own, the gates are never closed.

Moshe displayed this kind of weeping (*Shemot* 2:6): "...and behold, it was [like] a youth (*na'ar*) crying." The Malbim explains that he was crying in the manner of a youth, uninhibited and spontaneous, and so Pharaoh's daughter had pity on him.

It says about Yosef (*Bereishit* 43:30), "Yosef hurriedly [turned aside], for his compassion toward his brother was aroused and he wished to cry." Weeping that emanates from deep emotion has the potential to arouse one's inner self. Tears have the power to calm a person if they are accompanied by self-awareness.

In the generation of the desert, we see an example of weeping for improper motives (*Bemidbar* 14:1). Their weeping, which emanated from ungrateful self-pity and despair, became a cause of mourning for future generations.

Our Matriarch Rachel also wept, and Hashem comforted her. "So says Hashem: Stop your voice from weeping and your eyes from shedding tears, for there is a reward for your actions." Rachel, whose entire life was one of supreme self-sacrifice, who gave up her beloved for the sake of her sister, was pure of all personal bias. She merited that her tears rose to the heavens and evoked great mercy, which will be the trigger for Israel's ultimate redemption. One is capable of such exalted weeping after a lifetime of toil for one goal only: to do the Creator's will.

We also learn from King David (*II Shemuel* 12:21):

> And his servants said to him... "While this child was living, you fasted and wept; but now that he is dead, you arise and eat bread?" and he said, "While the child was still alive, I fasted and wept, for I said, 'Perhaps Hashem will be gracious to me and let the child live.' But now that he is dead, why should I fast? Can I yet bring him back? I am going to him but he will not return to me."

King David's faith in Hashem was so great that as long as his child was still alive, he fasted and prayed, but after HaKadosh Baruch Hu decreed death on the child, King David accepted the decree with such love and perfection that he was immediately able to get up and eat.

Look at the wonderful words that he said to his servants: "*I am going to him* but he will not return to me." Only a person who has humbled himself and keeps the day of his death uppermost in his mind, who truly feels "I am going to him" — I am already on the way right now — instead of "I will go to him one day" — only such a person has the strength to accept God's decree with love, and straightaway rise and eat. This attitude implies one's absolute vindication of the Heavenly judgment.

Sometimes we cry during prayer while making a request for the future. For instance, Chanah cried for a child, promising to dedicate him to the service of Hashem. Her weeping was not for herself, but emanated from deep devotion to the Jewish people.

WHAT DOES IT MEAN THAT man is made in the image of God?

Rav Shimon ben Rav Tzemach Duran (the Rashbatz) writes in *Magen Avot*:

> Hashem has elevated man above the animals by creating him in His image. It was not said of any other creature that it was created in the image of *Elokim*, since man is capable of recognizing his Creator more than other creatures are. Because of this, he is called "the image of God," for he is the choicest of all images.

Man is beloved to Hashem because he was created in His image. Since HaKadosh Baruch Hu loves mankind, He equipped him with special qualities and talents, which elevate him over the entire Creation.

The word *tzelem*, "image" (צלם), contains the letters of the word *tzel* "shade" (צל), darkness, suggesting something hidden, hinting that man is graced with the intelligence to discover the hidden powers of the soul. If he so seeks, he will discover many such powers.

A person has powerful contradictory strengths — his godly intelligence and his physical power.

The Torah teaches a person how to use these powers and how to strive for perfection. Fortunate is one who knows how to study the Torah and fulfill its guidelines.

A Righteous Man Who Suffers;
A Wicked Man Who Enjoys a Good Life

> *Avraham asked for old age.*
> *Yitzchak asked for sufferings.*
> *Yaakov asked for illness.*
> *(Yalkut Shimoni, Chayei Sarah 108)*

IT'S VERY STRANGE. People think that old age, suffering, and illness are bad things — why then did these *tzaddikim*, our Patriarchs, seek these things for themselves, and why were they given them?

Rav Dessler explains: Avraham, Yitzchak, and Yaakov felt that they were lacking these important tools in their service of Hashem. He explains the meaning of this at length (*Michtav Me-Eliyahu*, vol. 3, p. 187).

We learn from this that what we consider bad is not necessarily considered bad by *tzaddikim* who yearn to perfect their service of Hashem. It's a wondrous thing! Can mere human beings like us measure such things?

The Master of the World, Who knows all generations in advance, is perfect in all that He does. How then can such things be questioned? The matter can be compared to a very ill man whose child calls the doctor. The doctor arrives and begins to treat the father. The agonizing treatment requires making an incision, and the father cries out in pain. The child protests to the doctor, and asks him to put away his instruments and stop "hurting" his father. Who is right — the doctor or the child?

An amazing story is told about the Kaliver Rebbe. Rav Yitzchak Eizik of Kaliv suffered pain all his life, but he accepted it all with courage and with love for his Maker. Once, one of his doctors asked him, "Rebbe, how can you bear such constant suffering?"

The Rebbe replied, "I have a special method: I tell myself that my past sufferings no longer hurt. As for my sufferings in the future, they certainly don't hurt, and there's no point in worrying about them now. So what's left? Only the sufferings of the present, and they only last a second!"

Our Sages have compared suffering to a ship. Just as a ship without cargo will be spun around by the wind, will not reach its destination, and may even capsize, so it is with a man: If his life is too pleasurable, and everything is going too well, in the end he may, God forbid, rebel. So the burden of sufferings, his "cargo," is given to him to keep him on a straight course.

Despite this, we should all pray that God will treat us with mercy and teach us the right way without heavy afflictions, since it is very difficult to withstand them.

It is said that the *Shechinah* also suffers when we are in pain, as it says, "I am with him in suffering" (*Tehillim* 91:15). There were righteous men who used to weep for the *Shechinah*'s anguish even more than for their own.

Rabbi Nachman of Breslav writes that when a person takes the time to converse with Hashem, to tell Him of his suffering, to confess his sins, and to show regret for the many blemishes that he has made, then the *Shechinah* also addresses *him*, tells him of her suffering, and consoles him — for every blemish that he made upon his own soul also caused, so to speak, a blemish upon the *Shechinah*.

THE LUBAVITCHER REBBE SAID:

> Joy breaks through the fence of external limitations that surrounds the root of a man's soul. Joy reaches his intrinsic self, the essence of his soul.

Joy brings one to a Godly revelation.

Prayer is essential. There is tremendous power in prayer. We see this in Moshe's prayer for his sister Miriam (*Bemidbar* 12:13): "God! Please! Please heal her!"

The Midrash explains:

> At that time, HaKadosh Baruch Hu told the ministering angels, "Go down quickly and lock the Heavenly gates against Moshe's prayer. His prayer is like a sword that can cut through anything."

This short prayer had the efficacy of a sharp sword, for Moshe said it in complete concentration. It was like an arrow aimed at a target that hit the bull's-eye. Such is the power of prayer that is said from the depths of one's heart.

But it is not only great people like Moshe who are capable of such effective prayers. We learn this from the wicked Esav. Our Sages say, "The two tears that Esav shed granted him Mount Seir and the power of the sword."

When a person prays, he connects with HaKadosh Baruch Hu's will, and then HaKadosh Baruch Hu's abundance flows down to him directly, with nothing intervening.

HaKadosh Baruch Hu longs for our prayers.

Prayer

Teach me what to speak to You.
Show me what I should say to You.
Let me know what I should cry out to You.
Show mercy to a wretched person like me
To a lame-hearted person like me
To an ignorant and foolish person like me
To a feeble person like me
To a confused, addled, distracted person like me.
For the good that is in me is shackled in prison,
In a very great and bitter exile.

(R' Nachman of Breslav)

The bottom line is: We must rely on our Creator. The One Who created us knows our strengths, provides for our needs, and gives us our place in This World.

Epilogue

WHEN I FINISHED WRITING this book, I read through it several times, and each time I discovered various topics that were not adequately covered. It seems to me that a narrow personal view cannot adequately cover this important topic. It's impossible to go in-depth, and it's certainly difficult to find solutions for every question and ache that arises.

But I did what I could, and said whatever I felt had to be said. I would be pleased to hear from people who went through a crisis in their life and managed to overcome it. I ask this for the sake of the public and for the sake of individuals, since the more material there is, the more people can read and help each other.

My dream is to study the subject of bereavement, and then to set up a body headed by people with warm Jewish hearts. This body will offer support to people going through a crisis. It will present programs, including workshops offering various activities, and will instruct health trainees on how to help children who are suffering.

In the meantime, to my sorrow, I have heard many stories about people who plummeted as a result of their bitter fate.

It is very difficult to deal with the education and upbringing of orphan children. Because of their extreme sensitivity, they need ongoing guidance and advice.

I would appreciate hearing from one and all. Please write to me at:

"Sha'alei Tzion"
POB 7318
Jerusalem, Israel

Phone and fax: 972-2-5669696.

Brachah

Glossary

The following glossary provides a partial explanation of some of the Hebrew words and phrases used in this book. The spellings and explanations reflect the way the specific word is used herein. Often, there are alternate spellings and meanings for the words.

ABBA: Father, Daddy.
A"H: a Hebrew acronym for "May peace be upon her."
AKEIDAT YITZCHAK: the Binding of Isaac (see *Genesis*, chapter 22).
AVRAHAM AVINU: Abraham our father.

BA'AL TESHUVAH: a formerly non-observant Jew who becomes religiously observant.
BARUCH HASHEM: "Thank God."
BEIT HAMIKDASH: the Holy Temple in Jerusalem.
BEIT MIDRASH: lit., "house of study"; the study hall of a yeshiva or synagogue.
BEN TORAH: one who is devoted to Torah.
B'EZRAT HASHEM: "With God's help."
BIKKURIM: [the offering of the] first fruits.
BRIT [MILAH]: the covenant [of circumcision].

CHAS V'SHALOM: "God forbid!"
CHATAN: a groom.
CHAVRUTA: (A.) a Torah study partner.
CHAZAL: a Hebrew acronym for "our Sages of blessed memory."
CHESED: lovingkindness.
CHILLUL SHABBAT: desecration of the Sabbath.
CHUMASH: the Five Books of Moses.
CHUPPAH: a wedding canopy; also, a canopy honoring the righteous in Paradise.

CHUTZPADIK: (Y.) brash, disrespectful.

DAYAN: a judge in a Jewish court of law.

DIVREI TORAH: short presentations of Torah thoughts.

ELOKIM: the name for God in His attribute of judgment.
EMUNAH: faith.

GAN EDEN: the Garden of Eden.

GAON: a genius in Torah learning.

GEMACH: a Hebrew acronym for *gemilut chassadim* (benevolence); a free-loan society.

GER TZEDEK: a righteous convert.

HAKADOSH BARUCH HU: the Holy One, Blessed is He, i.e. God.

HALACHOT: Jewish laws.

HASHEM: God.

HAVDALAH: lit., separation; the ceremony marking the conclusion of the Sabbath and Festivals, separating the holy day from the other days of the week.

IMMA: Mother, Mommy.

IM YIRTZEH HASHEM: "God willing."

KALLAH: a bride.

KIDDUSH: the sanctification of the Sabbath and Festivals, usually recited over a cup of wine or grape juice.

KIPPAH/KIPPOT: skullcap(s).

KLAL YISRAEL: the community of the people of Israel; the Jewish nation.

KOLLEL: a center for advanced Torah learning for adult students, mostly married men, who receive stipends for their studies.

KOTEL: the Western Wall.

LECHEM MISHNEH: the two loaves of bread placed on the Sabbath table.

MA'ARIV: the evening prayer service.

MASHIACH: the Messiah.

MEGILLAH: a scroll; usually refers to the Book of Esther.

MEGILLAT EICHAH: the Book of Lamentations, which is traditionally read on TISHAH B'AV.

MEHUDAR: especially beautiful.

Glossary

MEZUZAH: a small scroll containing verses from the Book of *Deuteronomy* affixed to the doorpost (see *Deuteronomy* 6:9).

MINCHAH: the afternoon prayer service.

MINYAN: a quorum of ten adult Jewish males needed for communal prayer.

MISHNAYOT: the codified Oral Law, redacted by Rabbi Yehudah HaNasi; specific paragraphs of the Oral Law.

MITZVAH/MITZVOT: commandment(s).

MOHEL: one who performs the ritual of circumcision.

MOSHAV: a rural agricultural settlement.

MOTZA'EI SHABBAT: "the departure of the Sabbath" – Saturday night.

NACHAT: pride, pleasure.

NER NESHAMAH: a memorial candle lit for a deceased person.

PAROCHET: the curtain in front of the Holy Ark in the synagogue.

RACHEL IMMENU: our matriarch Rachel.

RAV: a rabbi.

RIBONO SHEL OLAM: Master of the World, i.e. God.

ROSH CHODESH: the first day of the Hebrew month.

SEFER/SEFARIM: book(s); holy book(s).

SEFER TORAH: a Torah scroll.

SEUDAH SHELISHIT: the third Sabbath meal.

SEUDAT MITZVAH: a festive meal held in honor of a MITZVAH such as a wedding or a BRIT MILAH.

SHABBAT: the Sabbath.

SHACHARIT: the morning prayer service.

SHALOM ALEICHEM: "May peace be with you," a traditional Jewish greeting.

SHECHINAH: the Divine Presence of God.

SHEMITTAH: the Sabbatical year.

SHIVAH: lit., seven; the first seven days of mourning.

SHLITA: a Hebrew acronym for "May he live long."

SIDDUR: the prayer book.

SOFER STAM: a scribe who writes Torah scrolls, TEFILLIN, and MEZUZAHS.

SUKKAH: a temporary dwelling in which Jews live during the Festival of Sukkot.

TAHARAH: lit., purification; the process of ritually purifying a deceased person before burial.

TALLIT: a prayer shawl.

TEFILLIN: small leather boxes containing Torah passages written on parchment, and worn by men during weekday prayers.

TEHILLIM: [the Book of] Psalms.

TISHAH B'AV: the ninth day of the Hebrew month of Av, which is a fast day commemorating the destruction of the two Temples.

TU BI'SHEVAT: the fifteenth day of the Hebrew month of Shevat.

TZADDIK: a righteous and holy person.

TZEDAKAH: charity.

TZITZIT: fringes knotted in a special way and affixed to four-cornered garments worn by males to remind them of God and His commandments.

VIDUY: the confessional prayer.

YEKKE: a German Jew; figuratively, a person characterized by punctuality and precision.

YEREI HASHEM: those who fear God.

YOM TOV: a Jewish Festival.

Z"L: a Hebrew acronym for "May his memory be for a blessing."

ZT"L: a Hebrew acronym for "May the memory of a righteous person be for a blessing."

ZTVK"L: a Hebrew acronym for "May the memory of a righeous and holy person be for a blessing."